MW00659173

1

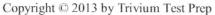

Printed in the United States of America

Table of Contents

Introduction 7

Chapter 1: Case Management Concepts 9

Chapter 2: Principles of Practice 55

Chapter 3: Psychosocial Aspects 73

Chapter 4: Healthcare Management and Delivery 87

Chapter 5: Healthcare Reimbursement 107

Chapter 6: Rehabilitation 123

Test Your Knowledge 137

Test Your Knowledge—Answers 173

Introduction

Congratulations! By reading this book, it means you have decided to advance your career in the medical field by becoming a Certified Case Manager. Before we get started, let's review some of the basic information. You are likely already familiar with this exam, the eligibility requirements, and so on, so we will keep it brief.

About the Exam

The Certified Case Management exam is created and administered by the CCMC, or Commission for Case Manager Certification. The exam takes about 3 hours and includes 180 multiple choice questions. 150 of the questions are scored, the other 30 are "pre-test" items and are not used in the scoring of your exam.

Eligibility Requirements

Per the CCMC, an applicant must:
- Be licensed or certified in one of the following manners:
  - Hold a current, unrestricted license in a discipline of health and human services. The scope of this license must allow the professional to conduct independent assessments.
  -OR-
  - A Bachelor's degree in nursing, social work, or another health/human services field.
- Have appropriate work experience at the time of application. Remember that employer verification is required, so ensure your information is accurate.
  - Category 1: 12 months of full-time case management experience supervised by board certified CCM.
  - Category 2: 24 months of full-time case management employment (supervision is not required in this category)
  - Category 3: 12 months full-time experience in case management as a supervisor of other individuals who provide case management services.

Applying for the Exam

To apply for the exam, you will need to visit the CCM website at www.ccmcertification.org. Everything you need to complete your application is located in the "My CCM Dashboard" section of the website. Keep in mind, you will need to upload a scanned copy of your current license/certification or an attestation of the degree you hold. There is a $160 non-refundable application fee, PLUS a $185 examination fee. The $185 examination fee is refundable should it be determined you are ineligible to take the CCM exam. If you require special accommodations, need to reschedule, need to defer, or want your exam re-scored, please contact the CCMC for assistance. There are fees associated with the different requests and accommodations.

Preparing for the Exam

Obviously, you are already off to a great start by reading this book! However, there are of course additional resources you should use as well. When you visit the CCMC website to apply for the exam, be sure to look through the free resources available there. You can see an outline or "blueprint" of the exam, which is very helpful to familiarize yourself with the general concepts you'll see on the test. This won't provide any detail about the concepts, so it's not useful for in-depth studying like you will get in this book, but is certainly a good idea to be familiar with the outline of the exam. The more you know about and are familiar with the exam beforehand, the better you'll do. They also provide a few sample questions, so is a good place to get an initial assessment of your current knowledge if you like (we have a lot of practice questions in this book too of course).

Chapter 1: Case Management Concepts

This section covers overview of case management; target patient populations; various roles and functions of case managers; purposes and goals of case management practice; case management models; the case management process; interpersonal communication; data interpretation and reporting; programs evaluation and research methods; case recording, documentation, and coding; quality and performance improvement concepts; conflict resolutions; acuity levels; and caseload calculation.

Overview of Case Management

According to the Case Management Society of America (CMSA, 2012), case management is "a collaborative process of assessment, planning, facilitation, care coordination, evaluation, and advocacy for options and services to meet an individual's and family's comprehensive health needs through communication and available resources to promote quality, cost-effective outcomes." Case managers use a set of logical steps and a process of interaction to ensure a patient receives necessary services in an efficient, supportive, and cost-effective way. There are numerous terms that are used to describe the case management process: care management, service management, care coordination, service coordination, and case coordination. Many agencies use the term care management instead of case management for the elderly, chronic, and long-term care patient populations (Lowery, 2008).

Case management practice began in the mid-1980s as a response to the prospective payment system in acute care. Today, case management models are used in almost every healthcare system and organization, regardless of the setting. Many people often confuse the terms *managed care* and *case management*. In general, managed care is systems-oriented, focusing on health insurance plans and the management of various benefits. Case management is people-oriented and focused on disbursement of managed care systems in a manner that benefits everyone, especially the patient (Powell & Tahan, 2010).

Principles of Case Management Practice

The five principles that serve as a basis of case management practice are:

1. Focus on patient and family
2. Negotiating, procuring, and coordinating services and resources
3. Use of the clinical reasoning process
4. Development of various relationships
5. Episode- or continuum-based (Cohen, 1996)

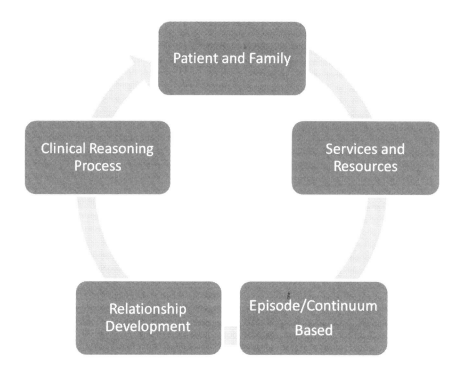

Target Patient Populations

With case management, patient selection criteria are determined by the employer of the healthcare facility. Populations are targeted for various conditions and reasons such as:

- Diagnostic categories – Acute injury or illness, chronic injury or illness, multiple diagnoses, and end-stage disease processes
- Potential for high utilization of resources – Financial and service
- Age and health status – Frail and elderly
- Procedure – Organ transplantation, cardiac surgery, and others
- Length of hospitalization – Frequent and/or prolonged hospitalizations and emergency room visits
- Psychological factors – Need for support system, financial resources, decision support, transportation issues
- Vocational support – Disability and loss of work
- Functional impairments – Paralysis, loss of a limb, need for ADL assistance
- Disability – Mental retardation and developmental disorders (Lowery, 2008)

Various Roles and Functions of Case Managers

The roles and functions of a case manager are defined by many professional organizations such as the American Nurses Association (ANA) and the Case Management Society of America (CMSA). Roles and responsibilities are documented in the healthcare facility's job descriptions, and they are based on the lessons learned from the implementation of case management programs. These roles and functions vary according to the setting in which the nurse works, the patient population being served, and the case management program and processes. They also differ based on a case mix of patients. Geriatric patients have different needs than pediatric patients, just as cancer patients have different needs than acutely ill patients (Powell & Tahan, 2010).

Six Domains of Case Management Roles and Functions

Case Finding and Intake

- Identification of patient who would benefit
- Obtainment of informed consent for services
- Communication of patient needs to others
- Identification of patients who need alternate levels of care

Provision of Services

- Facilitation and coordination of care activities
- Assumption of responsibility for communication with other healthcare providers
- Monitoring patient progress and care activities
- Review and modification of healthcare services
- Collaboration with stakeholders in a case management plan
- Serving as patient and family advocate
- Assuring adherence to various standards

Evaluation and Case Closure

- Data collecting, analyzing, and reporting
- Quality of case management services evaluation
- Access to timely and necessary services
- Application of evidence-based practice guidelines in plan
- Closing the case manager-patient relationship
- Reporting termination of services to stakeholders
- Educating patient regarding illness prevention

Utilization Management

A. Evaluation of appropriate level of care
B. Communication with payers and other healthcare providers
C. Allocation of resources based on patient needs
D. Management of reimbursement appeals and denials
E. Review of patient condition for appropriateness of hospitalization
F. Identification of cases that are at high risk for complications

Psychosocial and Economic Issues

- Review of patient's social and financial resources
- Assessment of patient's support network
- Consideration of patient's culture in planning and delivering care
- Evaluation of the ability of a caregiver outside the hospital setting
- Determination of eligibility for insurance coverage and/or charity services

Vocational Issues

A. Identification of need for changes in the home environment
B. Elimination of access barriers
C. Determination of need for specialized services
D. Arrangement for vocational assessment and services
E. Coordination of job analysis to implement modifications
F. Management of return-to-work activities (Powell & Tahan, 2010)

Role Dimensions

The Clinical-Patient Care Role Dimension

With the clinical-patient role dimension, nurse case managers are responsible for identifying existing or potential health problems by assessing the patient's physical, psychosocial, functional, financial, cognitive, and spiritual condition. Also, they develop a plan of care in collaboration with other healthcare providers of the interdisciplinary team. The plan of care consists of key tasks, treatments, or events required for the patient's care goals and of learning the needs of the patient and family. Nurse case managers often use prospectively developed protocols to meet the patient's needs. These protocols direct, monitor, and evaluate treatments and nursing interventions and communicate expected outcomes of the care plan (Tahan, 2005).

Typical Job Duties

- Discuss preventive services
- Direct patient care activities
- Assess the patient's and family's coping abilities, social support networks, and financial/insurance status
- Intervene when a problem is identified
- Facilitate patient progress through the healthcare system
- Arrange for consultations with specialists or specialty services
- Ensure transfer to appropriate level of care when necessary
- Collaborate with the interdisciplinary healthcare team (Tahan, 2005)

The Managerial-Leadership Role Dimension

The managerial-leadership role dimension refers to the case manager's duties for facilitating, coordinating, and expediting the care of patients while they are ill. Examples of these functions include scheduling and following up on tests, procedures, and treatments; patient and family teaching; negotiating community resources; and obtaining authorizations from the managed care agency. Case managers also must collaborate with the interdisciplinary team to determine the projected length of stay, the goals of treatment, and the necessary services (Tahan, 2005).

Typical Job Duties

- Evaluate the quality of care provided on a continual basis
- Conduct retrospective and concurrent chart reviews for utilization management
- Guide patient care activities and nursing interventions
- Facilitate communication among the members of the interdisciplinary team
- Serve as preceptor for case managers who are training (Tahan, 2005)

The Financial-Business Role Dimension

A case manager must ensure that the patient receives adequate care, while maintaining appropriate resource allocation through cost containment. This financial-business role dimension involves collaboration with other healthcare providers. To contain cost, the case manager must access information related to reimbursement methods such as *Current Procedural Terminology* (CPT) and diagnosis-related groups (DRGs). He/she determines the cost for each procedure based on diagnosis, the predetermined length of stay, and the necessary treatments. Then, the case manager must review resources and evaluate the efficiency of services related to the patient's diagnosis. To do this he/she must be familiar with healthcare reimbursement methods such as third-party reimbursement procedures, prospective payment systems, and operations of managed care organizations (Tahan, 2005).

Typical Job Duties

- Assess variances such as deviation from norms and delays in care
- Ensure continuity, integration, and coordination of care activities to control any duplication or fragmentation in care
- Access information on case mix indexes, practice patterns, and consumption of resources
- Ensure the use of necessary treatments and completed procedures within reimbursable time frames (Tahan, 2005)

The Information Management-Communication Role Dimension

With the information management-communication role dimension, the case manager uses applicable information to communicate, report, teach, reinforce, and evaluate situations and functions of the healthcare system. All roles and functions of the case manager depend on information sharing, and the information is directed toward achieving clinical and organizational outcomes, eliminating variances of care, and improving patient care. The success of the case management process depends on how well the case manager communicates with patients, families, healthcare providers, and payers. There are two types of stakeholders concerned with this role: internal (those involved with the interdisciplinary team) and external (managed care organizations) (Tahan, 2005).

Typical Job Duties

- Data collection and analysis of variances, quality assurance, and outcomes management
- Communicating and disseminating information through educational sessions, case conferences, reports, managed care reviews, and authorizations
- Report generation of case-managed patients, cost analysis, variances, denials and appeals, admission rates, and cost-benefit analysis
- Presentations by posters, public speaking, and storyboards
- Development and revision of policies and procedures
- Obtaining authorizations for services from various managed care organizations
- Reporting findings of utilization review and management activities (Tahan, 2005)

The Professional Development-Career Advancement Role Dimension

Professional development and advancement are both important for nurse case managers. With the professional development-career advancement role dimension, the nurse gains the confidence and support of members of the interdisciplinary team. There are many advantages for maintaining membership in professional organizations related to case management. This allows the nurse to network with other case managers to exchange information related to the latest technologies in the field and to obtain professional support. Also, the case manager can maintain professional practice standards and promote ethics-based practice. Finally, professional organization membership allows the case manager to have a political voice to advocate for health and to make public policy changes (Tahan, 2005).

Typical Job Duties

- Conduct research and utilize research findings
- Promote evidence-based practice
- Advocate for patients and families
- Share information at public forums
- Train novice case managers
- Participate in continuing education

- Remain up-to-date with the latest healthcare innovations and practices (Tahan, 2005)

Purposes and Goals of Case Management Practice

The goals and objectives of case management are the same, regardless of the practice setting. Also, there are many reasons for the use of case management services. A case manager serves in many roles and has numerous responsibilities.

Purposes

Several reasons why healthcare facilities use case management are:

- To maximize efficiency of valuable and available resource usage
- To promote informed decision-making by the patient and others by interjecting objectivity and information
- To work with the patient and with the family, physician, and other healthcare providers to implement a plan of care that meets the patient's needs
- To make the healthcare delivery system more effective
- To assist the patient in meeting planned outcomes through appropriate interventions and with a measurable process
- To promote safe, cost-effective, accessible, and quality care
- To assist patients and families in arranging and managing the complex resources required to maintain independent functioning and adequate health (Lowery, 2008)

Goals

The goals and objectives of case management are the same, regardless of the practice setting. They are:

- To promote the patient's wellness, autonomy, and appropriate use of financial resources and services
- To assist the patient to achieve an optimal level of functioning and health by facilitating and coordinating appropriate healthcare services
- To assist the patient to self-direct care, self-advocate, and make informed decisions
- To ensure that services are provided in a cost-effective and timely manner
- To facilitate the organization with appropriate sequencing of healthcare services in the most cost-effective way without compromising the quality of care
- To help the patient maintain the highest level of independence and human dignity and to enable them to reside in the most appropriate environment
- To provide a comprehensive and coordinated response to the patient's' needs that addresses rehabilitation, maintenance, and prevention

- To improve patient safety, satisfaction, productivity, and quality of life
- To provide quality healthcare along a continuum that decreases fragmentation of care
- To promote humane operation of systems that provide patients with resources, opportunity, and services (Lowery, 2008)

Case Management Models

Case management models are used in every phase of managed care and in every setting of healthcare delivery. These models are categorized as one of two approaches: within-the-walls and beyond-the-walls. Within-the-walls case management models are implemented in the acute care setting, and they focus on managing the care of patients during an acute illness. Beyond-the-walls case management models are implemented in settings other than acute care such as community, long-term care, and outpatient. The case manager's role depends on the setting. With within-the-walls models, he/she is involved with transitional and discharge planning, whereas with beyond-the-walls models, he/she is focused on rehabilitative and supportive care (Powell & Tahan, 2010).

Acute Care Management Model

Acute care case management involves time-limited, episodic nursing case management at the hospital level. The nurse case manager may also provide hands-on care of the patient, identifying acute care needs and discharge requirements in addition to developing the treatment plan along with members of an interdisciplinary team. This can be managed in one of the following five ways:

- Unit-based – Case manager manages patients while on a specific unit
- Complete-based – Case manager follows patients from admission to discharge
- Disease-based – Case manager following patients according to illness
- Practice-based – Case manager follows patients according to the physician
- Primary-based – Case manager is the primary nurse for certain patients (Powell & Tahan, 2010)

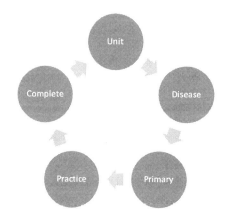

Primary Nurse Case Management Model

Primary nurse case management is based on the concept of managed care. With this model, the services and caseloads of the nurse case manager are designated for specific patient case mixes or types. Examples of case types include cardiac patients, cancer patients, stroke patients, and so on. The nurse is the primary caregiver for these patients, coordinating the care throughout hospitalization, regardless of the patient's physical location. The process of care is coordinated with group practice arrangements across geographic units and through healthcare team meetings. The nurse uses case management plans, which include critical pathway reports, DRG length of stay, and variance analysis. Additionally, patient discharge is planned before admission and updated throughout the hospitalization (Woodall, 2005).

Leveled Practice Model

The leveled practice model focuses on the management and coordination of patient care needs. It is a system that varies from the primary nurse case management model because the case manager focuses on the management activities of patient care instead of the delivery of the patient's care. The leveled practice model relies on information related to hospital costs, case mix, insurance, patient resource usage, and reimbursement. This model promotes differentiated practice arrangements by delineating the accountability and responsibility between nurses with baccalaureate degrees and those with associate degrees (Woodall, 2005).

The nurse case manager in the leveled practice model is responsible for monitoring the patient care of several assigned patients (the caseload) through collaboration with the patient, family, staff, and interdisciplinary team. Additionally, he/she focuses on mentoring, teaching, and coaching activities and on quality care improvement, patient outcome assessment, administration, and fiscal support (Woodall, 2005).

Emergency Department Case Management Model

With the emergency department case management model, case managers provide gatekeeping oversight to this area of the hospital. The case manager interacts with physicians, nurses, admitting office staff, payer-based case managers, and social workers to ensure medically necessary care that is cost effective. Numerous groups of patients are involved such as those admitted to the hospital; those who are treated and released; and those who are discharged, but require home care or other services. The case manager is involved in patient care mainly on the social level such as in cases dealing with abuse or homelessness (Powell & Tahan, 2010).

Admission Office Case Management Model

With the admission office case management model, the admitting office has a case manager who evaluates a patient prior to admission. This involves assessing the reasons for admission and setting up a preliminary plan of care. The main focus of this assessment is the patient's severity of illness and intensity of services. When a patient does not meet criteria for admission to the hospital setting, the case manager is responsible for diverting that patient to an alternate level of care. Also, admission office case managers contact the physician to discuss the findings of the assessment and to decide on a treatment plan. This model has been effective in reducing the number of reimbursement denials (Powell & Tahan, 2010).

Large Case Management Model

With the large case management model, the case selection includes patients who are at risk for high healthcare costs such as those with AIDS, premature infants, or spinal cord injury. Numerous settings support this model including hospitals, rehabilitation facilities, insurance companies, and home health agencies. This model focuses on patients with chronic illness, those with disabilities, and those who require intensive long-term care management and services. The nurse case manager's main focus is rehabilitation, both physical and vocational; prevention of deterioration in the health condition; and management of available healthcare resources (Powell & Tahan, 2010).

Disease Management Model

The disease management model continues to evolve, with case managers focusing on the natural course of a condition and on various treatment alternatives with attention to quality of care and cost. It is often used in clinical practices such as when identifying patients with diabetes and encouraging them to attend education classes or when distributing materials to women who need Pap smears. Additionally, disease management programs must be in sync with the needs of the healthcare facility. This involves using a planning framework and understanding program goals (Lind, 2005).

Elements of the Disease Management Model

- Understanding the course of the disease
- Targeting patients who would benefit from a particular intervention
- Focusing on resolution and prevention
- Providing care continuity across various healthcare settings
- Increasing patient compliance with education
- Establishing data management systems (Lind, 2005)

Some illnesses and conditions are more suitable than others for disease management. While chronic conditions account for around 80% of healthcare costs, these illnesses often show a more rapid return on investment than preventive healthcare. Specific elements that must exist before a condition is selected for disease management include sharing of real-time patient care data, patient education for self-care, and the ability to influence the continuum of care to lower costs and improve outcomes. The case manager must identify one or more clinical conditions that could improve patient care, shift utilization to a more appropriate level of care, and/or decrease health costs (Lind, 2005).

Insurance Case Management Model

Also called third-party payer case management model, the insurance case management model is based on the concept that quality of care and patient advocacy must be balanced with the responsibility for careful use of the health insurance plan's dollars. The case manager must resolve any conflict of expectations between the insurance company and the healthcare facility. This requires the use of communication and negotiation skills, where the case manager serves as the insurance company's liaison. The main focus with this model is managing members' benefits effectively and ensuring patients receive the necessary healthcare services in the most appropriate setting (Powell & Tahan, 2010).

Case managers who use the insurance case management model perform their job duties either by telephone or on-site. When done telephonically, case managers for large insurance companies use the telephone review process for assessment and planning. These professionals must be skilled in extracting the necessary information from the healthcare facility, which includes asking tough, but pertinent questions. With on-site management, the case manager reviews the patient's medical record, interviews members of the healthcare team, and assesses the patient's health. Regardless of whether the case manager performs his/her role on-site or telephonically, the focus is the same (Powell & Tahan, 2010).

Palliative Care Case Management Model

The palliative care case management model involves coordination of the care and comfort of dying patients and their families. The primary manager is the nurse case manager who works with the physician (the consultant). The focus of this model is the respectful and dignified care of patients suffering from terminal illness who have a limited life expectancy. Palliative care and hospice care deal with end-of-life. The case manager handles the complex consequences of the condition as the patient's death draws near. Also, the case manager assists with post-death issues that occur during the family's bereavement stage. Palliative care usually takes place in a home setting or in a skilled nursing or hospice facility (Powell & Tahan, 2010).

Home Health Case Management Model

The basic concept of the home health case management model is that case managers service the needs of chronically ill patients in the home setting. This involves coordination of many therapeutic modalities such as infusion therapy, wound care, physical therapy, occupational therapy, speech therapy, tube feeding, medication monitoring, and coordination of durable medical equipment. The home health case manager must monitor for early warning signs regarding the medical condition and contact the primary physician for treatment if problems occur. This way, the nurse can prevent or lessen the severity of exacerbation of illness and can reduce the need for hospitalization. The home health case manager's relationship begins with insurance authorization. Before services end, the nurse can extend authorization from the insurance company if credible reasons exist and if the case manager is adept in negotiation (Powell & Tahan, 2010).

Skilled Nursing Facility Case Management Model

With the skilled nursing facility case management model, the nurse case manager acts as a liaison between the acute care and sub-acute care levels. When a patient does not have adequate self-care abilities, skilled nursing facility placement is often necessary. Nurses who work in this environment assist the patient during the convalescent period by assessing the patient's condition and determining appropriate services. Many federal reimbursement changes have occurred and continue to occur. This has significantly increased case management opportunities (Powell & Tahan, 2010).

Community-Based Case Management Model

Also called the public health case management model, the community-based case management model is based on the concept of helping patients and families access appropriate services for independent functioning. Examples of community health nursing include Indian reservations, health departments, and low-income maternal/child health. Certain populations that need case managers include homeless families, substance abuse patients, mental health patients, and geriatric patients. Community-based case management works to prevent exacerbations of conditions through early assessment of the condition and through necessary interventions (Powell & Tahan, 2010).

Rehabilitation Case Management Model

The rehabilitation case management model embraces the concept of the case manager-social worker team. Rehabilitation units can be either free standing or in acute or sub-acute care facilities. These units accept patients for many reasons such as motor vehicle accidents, gunshot wounds, head trauma, spinal cord injuries, and cerebral vascular accidents. These patients function at a low enough level to require intensive rehabilitation services. Case managers in this environment work to bring the patient back to a functional level that is close to the person's baseline level. He/she also must utilize both private and community resources to ensure the patient receives appropriate care (Powell & Tahan, 2010).

Independent/Private Case Management Model

Many nurse case mangers start their own business. They are known as case management consultants and may be contracted by patients, family members, insurance companies, and physicians. The terms *private* and *independent* refer to the absence of oversight by a managed care organization or healthcare facility. With independent case management, the nurse works with firms that are not a formal part of an insurance company or other health-related facility. Benefits of private and independent case management include increased flexibility and autonomy in decision-making, coordination of services, independent planning, greater income, and professional satisfaction (Cohen, 2005).

With the independent or private entrepreneurial case management model, the nurse needs good business skills and should be prepared to work autonomously. Also, the independent nurse case manager coordinates all aspects of care in a variety of settings. He/she works with patients who have funds to supplement private insurance. These nurses function in a dual advocacy role and are expected to deliver cost-effective care (Powell & Tahan, 2010).

Collaborative Case Management Model

Collaboration is a process that involves joint decision-making among numerous parties where these persons have a collective responsibility for outcomes. Collaborative case management models bring positive outcomes such as reduced cost with improved quality of care and increased patient and staff satisfaction. With this model, all members of the team are held accountable for various aspects of case management. Physicians and nurses identify patients who are a high risk for resource utilization. Also, nurses facilitate evidenced-based pathway development and ensure appropriateness of care measures. The nurse case manager must ensure transition of care and facilitate discharge. Social workers assume the primary responsibility for psychosocially complex patients such as those with little or no resources or support. The utilization manager works with the insurance company for precertification and recertification (Koenig, 2005).

To create a collaborative care model, a clearly stated vision is necessary. A vision communicates a common purpose, gives a picture of the future, and assists individuals to set aside differences to work together cooperatively. Also, team success depends on each person's ability to do his/her job and on everyone working together as a whole. A team charter helps define how team members will work together. The charter is composed of the purpose of the team, the scope of work, boundaries, ground rules, decision-making process, roles of all members, and meeting information (Koeing, 2005).

Medical-Social Case Management Model

The medical-social case management model focuses on the long-term care patient who is at-risk for hospitalization. The model involves resource utilization of services that are not usually covered by health insurance, but are necessary to maintain the patient in a home setting. The case manager oversees the care planning, assessment, coordination, and care monitoring processes. The case manager facilitates arrangements with direct healthcare service delivery (Cohen & Celesta, 2005).

The Case Management Process

According to Ortiz and Riipi (2005), case management is a process, not a person. The case management model chosen by an organization is selected by many factors and does not remain static. Program evaluation is an ongoing part of the case management process, and it results in modifications to meet patient, organization, and payer needs. Effective case management programs need to develop a mechanism to trend system issues such as variances. These issues affect many aspects of the case management process such as patient care, length of stay, and resource utilization. To accomplish this task, data must be formatted to identify areas of performance improvement activities, serve as a decision-making tool, and track team productivity.

The case management process uses several of the same components as the nursing process: assessment, planning, implementation, monitoring, and evaluation. With case management, however, the focus is much broader, with the nurse having to assess the patient's condition before the current illness or incident, determine if the current environment will meet his/her present needs, investigate how the needs will be met, and plan further care (Ortiz & Riipi, 2005; Powell & Tahan, 2010).

Stages of the Case Management Process

    A. Case selection
    B. Problem identification
    C. Case plan development and coordination
    D. Case plan implementation
    E. Case plan evaluation
    F. Case plan reassessment and reevaluation
    G. Case closure (Powell & Tahan, 2010)

Stage 1: Case Selection

The first step in the case management process is case selection. This involves selecting patients who would benefit from case management services. If a patient meets intensity of services (degree of resources and services required for care) and severity of illness (acuity and acuteness of condition), and if no major discharge barriers exist and no psychosocial or financial concerns arise, case management is not required. Those patients who do need a case manager include people with moderate or complex illnesses, comorbidities, discharge needs, and/or social and financial issues (Powell & Tahan, 2010).

General Indicators

Several general indicators are used to detect situations that may require case management services. These include:

- <u>Length of stay</u> – Longer than five days

- Hospital charges – Greater than $50,000
- Home environment – Lives alone
- Age – Older than 65 years
- Payer source – Has Medicare disability or no insurance
- Readmission – Within 15 days for the same problem
- Physician services – Those of trauma surgeons or geriatric specialists
- First-time mothers – Having a first child
- Diagnosis-related group (DRG) – A special diagnosis (Powell & Tahan, 2010)

Psychosocial Indicators

Certain behavioral, mental health, and substance abuse conditions may warrant a case management assessment. Red-flag indicators include:

- Unintentional overdose – Can result from a lack of knowledge about medication
- Intentional overdose – Suicide gestures
- Alcohol and drug abuse – The primary or secondary cause of admission
- Eating disorders – Includes anorexia nervosa, bulimia, or failure to thrive
- Chronic mental illness – Includes schizophrenia, psychoses, neurotic disorders, depression, bipolar disorder, and anxiety
- Alzheimer's disease and dementia – Any form of confusion and/or disorientation
- Noncompliance – Often requires frequent readmissions
- Behaviors – Uncooperative, aggressive, or manipulative behaviors
- Miscellaneous conditions – Munchhausen syndrome or Munchhausen syndrome by proxy (Powell & Tahan, 2010)

Socioeconomic Indicators

Some socioeconomic factors alert the case manager to a need for case management. These high-risk situations include:

- Homelessness
- Child abuse or neglect
- Elder abuse or neglect
- Violent crime
- Domestic violence
- Poor living environment – Inadequate housing, poor sanitation, and lack of utilities
- Lack of support systems – No known social or family support systems
- Out-of-area residence – Includes out-of-state and out-of-country
- Rural residence – Services are nonexistent or lacking
- Limited/no financial resources
- Limited/no health insurance

- Single parent status
- Repeated admissions to acute care
- Frequent emergency department visits (Powell & Tahan, 2010)

Stage 2: Problem Identification

After the selection process, the nurse case manager moves on to problem identification. Assessment determines patient needs and establishes plans during this stage. To direct the case manager to treatment options, care coordination activities, and resource utilization, much data collecting and analysis is done. During this stage, potential and/or actual problems are exposed and goals are set. Assessment is critical to the case management process because conditions, circumstances, and events affect the discharge plan. A complete evaluation of the data is necessary to provide an individualized management plan for the patient (Powell & Tahan, 2010).

Problem Identification Assessment Categories

The assessment categories for problem identification include patient history and demographics, current medical status, nutritional assessment, medication assessment, financial assessment, functional assessment, psychosocial assessment, and cultural and religious assessment (Powell & Tahan, 2010).

Patient History and Demographics

- General – Name, age, address, marital status, employment, language spoken, and educational level
- Medical history – Includes previous diagnoses, current diseases, childhood illnesses, serious and chronic illnesses, accidents, and injuries
- Complicating factors – Chronicity and comorbidities
- Noncompliance issues
- Family history – Includes cancer, diabetes, heart disease, hypertension, and others
- Allergies – Includes food, drug, and environmental (Powell & Tahan, 2010)

Current Medical Status

- Interviewing healthcare providers – Includes physical, speech, and occupational therapists; home health nurses; social workers; assistants; and homemakers
- Reviewing data – Includes diagnostic test results, laboratory test results, vital signs, progress notes, physician reports, and other documents of observation
- Assessing utilization review modalities – Includes critical pathways, severity of illness criteria, and intensity of service criteria (Powell & Tahan, 2010)

Nutritional Assessment

- Inadequate food intake – Examine the frequency, amount, and quality of food choices
- Financial issues – That affect ability to purchase quality and sufficient amounts of food
- Social isolation – Depression can affect appetite
- Dental and mouth problems – Tooth and gum disease affects food intake
- Disability – Inability to shop for food and/or prepare food
- Weight loss – Strongly associated with decreased food intake
- Acute and chronic diseases – Numerous illnesses affect diet and appetite (Powell & Tahan, 2010)

Medication Assessment

- Allergies – Cannot take medication due to adverse effects
- Polypharmacy – Can affect physical and mental health
- Noncompliance – Not taking medication
- No transportation – Cannot obtain medication
- Financial issues – Cannot purchase medication
- Insurance issues – Insurance does not cover medications
- Laboratory monitoring – Includes chemotherapy, anticoagulants, and anti-lipid agents
- Ineffective route – To assess the most effective route of the medication
- Dosing – To see if medication is prescribed at the lowest effective dosage
- Containers – To see if medication containers are accessible
- Education deficits – To see if the patient understands instructions regarding medications (Powell & Tahan, 2010)

Financial Assessment

- Insurance coverage – Inadequate or no healthcare insurance
- Governmental entitlement – Includes Medicare, Medicaid, Supplemental Security Income (SSI), and Social Security Disability (SSD)
- Extra insurance costs – Copayments and deductibles
- Items not covered by insurance – Includes medications, supplies, and other items
- Financial obligations – Includes rent, utilities, and food (Powell & Tahan, 2010)

Functional Assessment

- Stairs – Can the patient use stairs?
- Telephone – Can the patient see and hear to use the telephone?
- Toilet, tub, and shower – Can the patient access these facilities?

- <u>Utilities</u> – Does the patient have adequate heating, air conditioning, and running water?
- <u>Sanitation</u> – Are there roach or rodent problems? Are there clean living conditions?
- <u>Equipment</u> – Does the patient have adequate durable medical equipment (DME)?
- <u>ADLs</u> – Can the patient perform activities of daily living?
- <u>Transportation</u> – Can the patient get to the store, pharmacy, and doctor?
- <u>Communication</u> – Can the patient see, hear, and speak English?

Psychosocial Assessment

- <u>Stresses</u> – What stresses are in the patient's family life during the illness?
- <u>People in the home</u> – Who is in the home?
- <u>Exhaustion and burn-out</u> – Can respite care be provided?
- <u>Hobbies and recreation</u> – Does the patient do things he/she enjoys?
- <u>Formal support system</u> – Is this system inadequate or dysfunctional?
- <u>Cognitive and mental status</u> – Is the patient alert and oriented?

Cultural and Religious Assessment

- <u>Gestures</u> – Includes non-verbal body language
- <u>Language barriers</u> – Misunderstanding of language and inability to speak English
- <u>Cultural traditions and taboos</u> – Includes eye contact, casual touching, and silence
- <u>Religious and spiritual beliefs</u> – Includes assessing the feasibility of pastoral and other church leader visits, reading materials, and videos
- <u>Cultural and religious conflicts</u> – Involves conflicts that exist with the patient (Powell & Tahan, 2010)

Stage 3: Case Plan Development and Coordination

With the third stage, case plan development, the case manager chooses the best way to provide care. The interdisciplinary team must decide what needs to be done, how best to accomplish this, who will provide the services, when the next level of care will be provided, and how the patient and family can manage after discharge. The three main steps in this stage are:

- <u>Establishing Goals</u> – Most goals involve many smaller goals that must be first met for successful completion of the main goal. For instance, many objectives require several modifications in the home setting for the goal of home safety to be a reality. A transfer to a skilled nursing facility could involve finding the appropriate location, finding a physician who will follow the patient there, setting up necessary DME, transferring medical records, obtaining physician orders, and getting reports from the interdisciplinary team. This all must be done before the ultimate goal can be met, which is quality care and efficient use of resources.

- Prioritizing Needs and Goals – With the second step of case plan development, the case manager prioritizes needs and goals. Occasionally, the patient's or family's idea of a priority problem is not the same as the case manager's idea of a priority issue. Each person views life from his/her own perspective, so something one person cannot live without is a minor inconvenience to another person. Also, patients and/or families may disagree with assessed priority needs. For instance, an alert and oriented elderly man may insist on going home alone, while the case manager feels that a skilled nursing facility would be the best choice for his care.

- Service Planning and Resource Allocation – The third step in the case plan development process is service planning and resource allocation. Once priority goals are set, the case manager must fill in healthcare gaps, reduce duplication of services, and assess for deficits. To fund needed services, the nurse turns to medical insurance companies for medical necessity requests. Options for obtaining services include negotiating or finding charitable agency resources, community-based agencies, neighbors and friends, and religious groups (Powell & Tahan, 2005).

Stage 4: Case Plan Implementation

The case plan implementation stage is the where the plan is put into action. During this stage, the patient's needs have been linked with resources and services, and the patient and support systems agree with the case management plan. The objective of this stage is to maximize the well-being and safety of the patient while using the most necessary level of care. The chosen cost-effective setting should match the patient's needs, desires, capabilities, financial abilities, and health condition (Powell & Tahan, 2005).

The types of implementation of a case management plan are identified by essential issues of internal and external case management. Internal case managers are professionals who are employed by the healthcare facility. These case managers are often called on-site managers who provide "within-the-walls" case management. External case managers are professionals who work outside the healthcare facility such as health maintenance organization (HMO) case managers, third-party payer case managers, and private case managers (Powell & Tahan, 2005).

Stage 5: Case Plan Evaluation

The stage of case plan evaluation and follow-up ensures case continuity. The job responsibilities of the type of case management determine what is completed in the evaluation stage. Some post-discharge follow-up can be done by telephone or in person. This can be as minimal as one or two phone calls or visits, or it can involve an extensive rehabilitation transitional period. Many hospital case managers follow a patient in the hospital and after discharge. Home healthcare case managers often follow up on the patient and family in the home setting. With hospice case managers, the patients are followed from admission into the programs until death (Powell & Tahan, 2005).

Numerous events can occur after discharge. Necessary services could be overlooked, equipment could not arrive on time, questions could arise, or the insurance agency may not approve necessary services. Additionally, the family may have difficulties with medications or health plan coverage of necessary medicines, or they may not be able to afford the medications. With follow-up and evaluation, the nurse case manager can answer questions, reassure the patient and family, and prevent complications or readmissions (Powell & Tahan, 2005).

The CMSA lists six standards of care for the practice of case management. These are case identification and selection, problem identification, planning, monitoring, evaluating, and outcomes. Outcomes evaluation involves the case manager determining goals with the patient and family, the physician, and the multidisciplinary team. Sometimes, outcomes in case management are patient-related; other times, they are measured in terms of cost-effectiveness. Adequate case management outcomes involve both cost and quality (Powell & Tahan, 2005).

Stage 6: Case Plan Reassessment and Reevaluation

Until the case is closed, case management reassessing, monitoring, and reevaluating must continue. This is the review process that reveals changes in the patient's medical condition or hidden social circumstances that alter progression. The case management plan is refined, revised, and fine-tuned during this stage. With certain types of case management, the nurse case manager must monitor the payer and the patient. The details of a case may change so that the payer does not want to continue providing case management services. Also, some patients may qualify for Medicaid or Medicare, so the original third-party payer is no longer liable (Powell & Tahan, 2005).

Changes that Require Monitoring

- Changes in Medical Status – A change in medical status could mean improvement or deterioration. When there is a medical status change, the patient must be monitored for insurance authorization and utilization purposes. Things that can change along with this are intensity of service, severity of illness, and clinical pathways.

- Changes in Social Stability – When there is a life change that occurs during a patient's stay in the hospital, it can be more difficult than the actual illness. During the convalescent period, a patient could lose a home or apartment, significant others, or pets. Prompt use of social services and changes to the discharge plan may be necessary with changes in social stability.

- <u>Changes in Quality of Care</u> – Although standards of care represent the expected norm, accidents and oversights often occur. If an unfortunate incident takes place, it is best to consult risk management personnel.

- <u>Changes in Functional Capability</u> – Numerous conditions can affect mobilization and functional capacity such as orthopedic surgery, profound weakness, hemiparesis, and deep vein thrombosis. Case managers need to prevent prolonged hospitalization due to these factors by initiating physical therapy and restorative nursing.

- <u>Changes in Educational Needs</u> – Knowledge deficits regarding the disease process and treatment must be identified during the case management process. With reassessment, new educational needs can be identified.

- <u>Changes in Pain Management</u> – Because pain is a subjective experience for the patient, it is often a complex and controversial aspect of healthcare. The case manager should monitor and reevaluate a patient's pain status periodically to address this healthcare need.

- <u>Changes in Patient/Family Satisfaction</u> – Throughout the case management process, the nurse must reevaluate and monitor patient and/or family satisfaction. Sometimes, the patient and/or family perceive that the physician is not attentive; other times, the physician is reluctant due to the patient's and/or family's constant demands (Powell & Tahan, 2005).

Stage 7: Case Closure

Case closure and termination of case management services is challenging. Case managers should answer patient and family questions to alleviate any anxiety and concerns and should educate the concerned parties about the reason for case closure. Also, they should share the expectation of termination with the patient and family during the first stage of the case management process. Case management services are terminated for numerous reasons including:

- Request for termination by the patient, provider, or payer
- Patient is no longer eligible
- Change in patient's medical condition
- Goals have been met
- Death of the patient
- Case management program is discontinued
- Case management company closed
- Case manager retires, changes jobs, or relocates (Powell & Tahan, 2005)

Interpersonal Communication

One mandatory skill of the nurse case manager is communication. The ability to work well with people is among employers' top three skills they consider when hiring case managers. Communication is verbal, non-verbal, and written. The purpose of communication in case management is to inquire, inform, and persuade. A case manager can inquire through verbal or written communication and by phone or in person. Informational communication is a key component of case management transactions, and insurance companies must be updated and informed of patients' health conditions, progress, and treatment plans. Aside from the patient and family, the nurse case manager communicates with insurance companies, physicians, and other team members (Alabama Department of Public Health, 2013).

Verbal communication refers to spoken words. If the information is obtained, provided, and shared with ease, it enhances the communication process. Words should be kept simple and in the appropriate vernacular. The case manager should avoid using abbreviated names, technical jargon, and medical terminology that is unfamiliar to the patient or family. A successful case manager can synthesize and articulate information without the need for constant clarifications and explanations. Common difficulties of verbal communication include:

- Hearing impairment
- Language barriers
- Developmental, cognitive, and/or psychological impairment (Alabama Department of Public Health, 2013)

Communicating with the Interdisciplinary Team

When communicating with interdisciplinary team members, a case manager should react and respond only to facts instead of feelings to avoid confrontations and biased decision-making. Professional communication skills that facilitate team communication include active listening, asking questions to clarify rather than challenge someone's ideas, respecting others' opinions, and not interpreting others' statements or interrupting others to give unsolicited advice (Powell & Tahan, 2010).

Communicating with the Patient

When communicating with a patient, both non-verbal and verbal responses give the case manager useful information and can be of equal importance. When someone is not telling the truth or does not want to answer a question, he/she may look away, become tense, and/or remain silent. Therefore, information obtained during an interview should include not only the patient's factual responses, but also concerns, attitudes, and non-verbal responses. The case manager should attempt to ask open-ended questions whenever possible. Also, rephrasing a patient's statement and providing a list of options are two strategies that encourage the patient to give more detailed information (Powell & Tahan, 2010).

Interview Techniques

One of the essential case management skills is interviewing. Case managers must conduct an interview to obtain and provide information necessary for the case management process. These interviews are conducted face-to-face, by telephone, by email, or in writing. Some interviews involve only the case manager and the patient, but the family is often included. Preparation for the interview will ensure that the goals and objectives of the interview are met and that the flow of the process is organized and purposeful (Alabama Department of Public Health, 2013).

Strategies for Interview Preparation

- Know the purpose of the interview, what must be accomplished, and what the expected outcomes are.
- Outline the information that should be obtained and provided and collect all necessary forms before the interview process.
- Obtain education regarding the main facts and topics of the interview.
- Make an appointment for the interview to show respect and ensure that the patient and family will have time to prepare.
- Arrange the interview room for the comfort of the patient and attempt to minimize noise and distractions (Alabama Department of Public Health, 2013).

The Interview Process

- Greet the participants and introduce yourself and others present.
- Explain the relationship and/or role of all concerned parties.
- If you plan to take notes or write during the process, inform all participants of this.
- Use a conversational style, vary your questions, and attempt to ask open-ended questions when possible.
- Ask only one question at a time and save personal questions for the end of the interview.
- Keep the objectives of the interview in mind and avoid turning the process into a question-answer session.
- Show empathy and understanding and practice active listening.
- Give participants a chance to ask questions.
- Close the interview with a review of the information discussed and facts collected.
- Thank all participants for their time and assistance (Alabama Department of Public Health, 2013).

Negotiation Techniques

In today's evolving healthcare environment, resources are not readily available, benefits are declining or are difficult to obtain, and cost is a major concern for the patient, hospital, and insurance company. For these reasons, negotiation is a significant factor. Negotiation serves numerous purposes. It has the capacity to control costs and to gain medically necessary benefits for the patient. Negotiation can also help avoid chaos that commonly occurs when the patient's condition deteriorates after necessary services or equipment is denied. Also, negotiation allows case managers to learn by gathering necessary information that can lead to successful negotiations in the future (Powell, 2008).

Negotiation is a daily activity of the case manager, and it is used with patients, families, payers, care providers, vendors, and other agents. The purposes of negotiation are to:

- Allow concerned parties to reach an agreement
- Allow the case manager to control costs
- Gain medically necessary benefits for the patient
- Help avoid chaos
- Improve quality of care
- Improve communication (Powell & Tahan, 2010)

Types of Negotiators

The two types of negotiators are aggressive and cooperative. With the aggressive style, the negotiator uses psychological maneuvers such as threats and intimidation. If the case manager feels that he/she is being manipulated, he/she brings the case back to the facts. The aggressive negotiator will make extreme demands with few concessions and will bring up false issues. With the cooperative style, the negotiator attempts to establish and maintain trust. The cooperative negotiator establishes a common ground, is fair and objective, and shows respect for the opponent. The attitude of the cooperative style is "win-win" (Powell, 2008).

Weaknesses of Aggressive Negotiation

- Tension and mistrust increase the likelihood of misunderstanding.
- Aggressive negotiation reputation can harm future negotiation measures.
- Aggressive tactics are likely to result in failed negotiations.
- The trial rate for aggressive negotiators is more than double (Powell & Tahan, 2010).

Strengths of Cooperative Negotiation

- Promotes mutual understanding
- Produces an agreement in less time than with the aggressive approach
- Produces an agreement more frequently than with the aggressive approach
- Makes future negotiations easier (Powell, 2008)

Emotional Intelligence

When dealing with other people, a nurse case manager must possess emotional intelligence (EI). Also called emotional quotient (EQ), EI involves the skill and capacity to perceive, assess, and manage your emotions, those of others, and those of groups of people. When negotiating, nurse case managers must have the ability to enter into emotional states associated with a drive to succeed. Also, they must have the capacity to read and influence other people's emotions (Powell, 2010).

The Mayer-Salovey Model of Emotional Intelligence

This four-branch model divides EI abilities into four areas: perceive, use, understand, and manage emotions. In other words, the nurse case manager must have the capacity to accurately perceive the emotions of others, use emotions to facilitate thinking, understand emotional meanings, and manage his/her own or others' emotions (Powell, 2010).

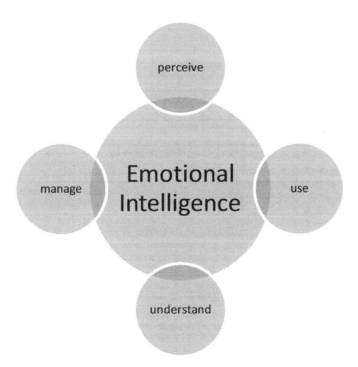

Data Interpretation and Reporting

Data is the recorded and reported measures or values of variables. They are either qualitative or quantitative measures in statistics or research. Data alone is not useful without a quantification framework. Statisticians classify data as parametric or nonparametric, related to the measurement level. Parametric data is observations on variables that represent the measurement of distance between points on a scale. They have consistent units and a uniform distribution of values. Two examples of parametric data are interval and ratio. Nonparametric data is not consistent and is considered distribution-free and arbitrarily measured. There is no uniform distance between units of measure. Examples are nominal and ordinal data (Barton & Skiba, 2005).

Five-Step Interactive Process Model

One model proposed to view the quantification process that leads to data-driven decisions is the five-step interactive process:

1. Thought – The initial step is characterized by curiosity and hypothesis.
2. Data – The second step is characterized by undigested observations.
3. Information – The third step is characterized by numbers put in useful form.
4. Knowledge – The fourth step is characterized by organized information.
5. Wisdom – In the final step, integrated knowledge is used for decision-making.

With case management, the nurse must collect, organize, move, and represent information. With processing, the nurse must transform the data to a more complex state of information. Once the information progresses to knowledge, it allows the case manager to use this knowledge to make decisions (Cleveland, 1985).

Levels of Measurement

Level of Measurement	Definition	Data Type	Example
Nominal	Numerical naming where numbers do not represent a degree or quantity	Nonparametric	Ethnicity
Ordinal	Rank-ordered numbers	Nonparametric	Patient acuity
Interval	Equal differences between numbers represent equal differences in the variable	Parametric	Length of stay
Ratio	Numbers represent equal amounts to form an absolute zero	Parametric	Fahrenheit temperature scale (Cleveland, 1985)

Five Categories of Healthcare Data

There are five categories of healthcare data described by Stead (1991). These are:

1. Historical data – Concerning a particular patient, device, or thing

34

2. Encountered patient data
3. Subgroup data – Related to a specified set of events or patient population
4. Work-flow management data
5. Knowledge databases – Used in decision-making

In nursing, patient care data is the main concern, where atomic-level data is precise data captured in the course of clinical practice. From a nursing informatics perspective, the objective of moving data to knowledge is called "informatting." Quality improvement managers incorporate patient-level data along with financial and population-based data to make decisions. The case management plan involves data collection for interpretation and use, and it provides patient care data, resource utilization data, and length of stay (LOS) data (Barton & Skiba, 2005).

Data Management Issues

Validity is related to the meaningfulness of data, whereas reliability is related to the accuracy of data. Validity and reliability are two concepts used to measure data quality. With the Nursing Minimum Data Set (NMDS), there are 16 data elements that represent patient demographics and other service data. However, there are numerous vocabularies and classification schemes, but no single system represents what all nurses do (Barton & Skiba, 2005).

Data-based decision-making involved with case management requires the case manager to collect the right information to manage outcomes. Outcomes management is the improvement of patient outcomes through exemplary health practices and quality services. Also, outcomes management is a data-driven and assessment-based process. Because outcomes management involves assessment, sometimes, the data requires considerable time and effort to locate, collect, and organize. This difficulty can be addressed by use of the concept of a corporate database (Barton & Skiba, 2005; Meistrell and Schlehuber, 1996).

The second data management issue concerns collecting data at multiple levels within the healthcare facility. Gathering data at the patient level is necessary to perform testing of statistical assumptions. The challenge for case managers with outcomes projects is the lack of awareness of the difficulties in mixing levels of data, planning studies, and using available techniques (Batron & Skiba, 2005).

Two Database Types

The two database types are:

- Data warehouse – This is used by nurse managers and analysts for population-based management and contains financial and clinical data. The data in this database is trended, comparative, and aggregate.
- Data repository – This is designed to facilitate the healthcare provider's decision-making regarding each patient. The focus of this database is on

clinical and operational data that is available in real-time (Batron & Skiba, 2005).

Statistical Approach

The statistical approach is one traditional method for data interpretation and reporting. It uses statistical techniques to analyze data and uses standard graphing to present data. The questions generated by the decision-makers are linked to the statistical techniques. These decision-makers must understand the data and recognize various data sources to answer the questions. Statistical techniques use both descriptive and inferential tools on parametric and nonparametric data. Central tendency and variability are two measures utilized to describe aggregated data, and the level of data can be nominal, ordinal, interval, or ratio. The specific measures with interval data are standard deviation and mean, whereas the mode and range are the best measures for nominal data (Batron & Skiba, 2005).

Information Processing Approach

The information processing approach to data interpretation and reporting involves automating data analysis in an attempt to discover data in large databases. This is known as knowledge discovery in databases (KDD), and experts in this growing field have core disciplines from statistics and database management and have a desire to extract useful knowledge from the volumes of data in warehouses. Information processing is also called information harvesting, information discovery, data archeology, and data pattern processing (Batron & Skiba, 2005).

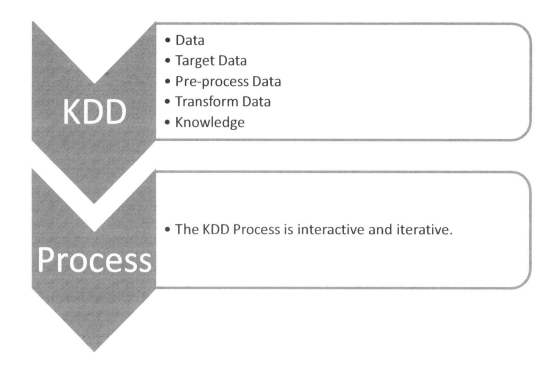

With the first step of the KDD process, the decision-maker learns about the data and objectives. The target data set or subset is created during the next step in the process. During the pre-processing step, the data is cleaned of items such as outliers. The fourth step involves transforming the data to reduce the effective number of variables. With the knowledge step, the data is mined for extraction of patterns or models of the data. Then, the decision-maker can interpret the findings, looking for redundancy and irrelevance. The user can draw conclusions from the data with the KDD process (Batron & Skiba, 2005).

Continuous Quality Improvement Approach

With the continuous quality improvement approach, data is reported by idea generation, portrayal of beliefs, display, and analysis. Idea generation includes boarding, decision matrices, and multi-voting. Portrayal of beliefs is done by flow and fishbone diagrams. Display is done with check sheets, run charts, and histograms. Finally, analysis is done with scatter diagrams and pie, Pareto, and control charts (Batron & Skiba, 2005).

Check sheets are used to record the frequency of an activity or incident such as tracking prolonged LOS reasons for a group of patients. A histogram is a bar chart that graphically presents data from the check sheet. A run chart shows observations over time to assess the temporal behavior of a process and to establish the time of process performance changes. This is done so these elements can be linked to the time of other related incidents. A control chart is much like a run chart, but it shows upper and lower control limits at three standard deviations. Pareto charts are used to show the significance of different factors, done similarly to the 80-20 rule, which compares 80% of the potential improvement to 20% of the issues (Batron & Skiba, 2005).

Program Evaluation and Research Methods

The success of a case management system is dependent on a well-conceived plan. Implementation is a nine-step process that requires program evaluation. The evaluation should occur at predetermined intervals, and necessary changes must be made along the way.

Implementing the Case Management Model

Assessing the system and creating an environment of change requires systematic planning and evaluation. When evaluating the case management model, the first step is determining if the program is not only feasible, but also worthwhile. Also, a thorough analysis, including financial and structural status, of the healthcare facility is required. A case management system can be implemented without extra personnel costs if the organization already employs competent people (Cohen & Cesta, 2005).

Internal Marketing

Part of the case management program's success is obtaining the support of senior management. The presentation of the model should include estimated costs, staffing needs, time frames, and a review of other organizations that have had success with the plan. The support of nursing administration is also critical to the program's success. Many nurse managers may feel threatened by the introduction of another individual who is also managing care (Cohen & Cesta, 2005).

Staff Integration

For the case management program to be successful, the administration must educate and obtain the full support of staff nurses. The role of the case manager in relation to other nursing positions needs to be clarified and reviewed with staff nurses. Also, most managed care and prospective payment systems offer no financial incentives to motivate physicians to discharge patients rapidly. Therefore, it may be difficult to obtain the support of physicians. Some managed care organizations give financial penalties to physicians for hospital days that extend the medically necessary length of stay. By denying payment to physicians, the managed care organization provides an incentive for the physician to be responsible for non-reimbursable days. Additionally, case management requires the support and cooperation of ancillary departments. To assist the case manager, a contact person in each department must be assigned (Cohen & Cesta, 2005).

Steps of Implementing the Case Management Model

- Step 1: Define Case Management Target Populations – The target patient populations are selected based on volume of discharges, variance from LOS standards, feasibility of case management plans, potential for resource consumption control, and opportunity to improve quality of care.

- Step 2: Define Target Areas – Patients are matched to appropriate clinical areas such as non-unit-based and unit-based. In some cases, the patients are matched to appropriate clinical areas, and in others, they are grouped according to geographic area.

- Step 3: Determine Design Structure – If a unit-based model is introduced, the facility must determine how many case managers will be on each unit. The healthcare providers change as the professionals assigned to the patient change, and for each new patient, the case manager must assemble a team. With a non-unit-based model, the team may need more resources for implementation. When the healthcare provider is taken away from other assignments, the vacancy must be filled by another person.

- Step 4: Form Collaborative Practice Groups – With the unit-based model, the teams have a fluid structure. With the non-unit-based model, the team members remain constant, and the changing member is the patient.

- Step 5: Choose Benchmarks – Benchmarks are selected early, and this method of evaluation depends on the outcome measures set for tracking data.

- Step 6: Collect Pre-implementation Data – The data collection method is determined, the time frames are set, and the individuals are identified. Some data is retrospective, and other data is real-time.

- Step 7: Provide Advanced Skills and Knowledge – The healthcare facility must offer an educational program regarding the case management system.

- Step 8: Implement the Model – The case manager works toward gradual change, communicating with other members of the healthcare team.

- Step 9: Evaluate the Model – Evaluation of the case management model involves data collection and analysis. Monthly evaluation should be done on certain data, LOS, and other important tracking elements. For staff and patient satisfaction, annual tracking is necessary. This evaluation process is ongoing and involves discussions with staff nurses and other healthcare providers (Cohen & Cesta, 2005).

End Outcomes of the Healthcare Case Management System

- High quality care – This is measured using proximate measures such as patient satisfaction questionnaires, readmission rates, morbidity and mortality, and complications.
- Appropriate or decreased costs – This is measured by reduction in hospital admissions, emergency department visits, or overall costs per case.
- Improved health status – This is measured using surveys or questionnaires that assess the patient's perception of the impact his/her health has on quality of life. Indicators include resumption of employment and absence of symptoms (Aliotta, 2005).

The Competency Outcomes and Performance Assessment Model

The Competency Outcomes and Performance Assessment (COPA) model was developed by Lenburg in 1991. To evaluate a program, this model uses an approach based on the performance abilities of various levels of employees. The COPA model contains a sequence of four components that guide the process of development, implementation, and evaluation of a case management program. These are:

1. Competency outcomes – What competency outcomes are necessary for actual practice? The broad performance-based competencies that are mandatory for

practice must be identified. These competencies define practice in broad categories and are the end result of learning and experience.

2. Practice skills and related actions – What specific practice skills and related actions provide sufficient evidence to represent competence in each category? This involves the unique skills and actions of key personnel and units. These skills and related actions define competence and are objective evidence of actual abilities.

3. Learning competencies – What are the best ways to learn these competencies? This includes the integration of actual practice expectations and the use of various learning strategies.

4. Evaluation of skills – What is the best method of assessing achievement of practice skills and related actions? To validate and document competence, the evaluator must have specific assessment methods, logistics, policies, and resources (Lenburg, 2005).

With the COPA model, the end result is considered the beginning. The preferred outcomes and essential practice abilities are clearly specified before they are learned, achieved, or evaluated. Specific methods of evaluation are developed to document achievement of actual performance. Therefore, it is necessary to start with the competency outcomes, regardless of their ambiguity (Lenburg, 2005).

COPA Model Concepts

The evaluation component of the COPA model is based on the 10 psychometrically based concepts:

- Examination
- Specified skills or dimensions of practice
- Critical elements that define competence for each skill
- Level of acceptability
- Sampling
- Objectivity
- Comparability
- Consistency
- Flexibility
- Systematized conditions (Lenburg, 2005)

COPA Model Core Practice Competencies

- Assessment and intervention skills – This includes all forms of assessment, data collecting, and monitoring and also therapeutic, technical, safety, managerial, and other intervention skills.

- Communication skills – This includes written, oral, and computer communication abilities that are commonly used to exchange information and send messages with or about patients, staff, the healthcare facility, and more.
- Critical thinking skills – This includes numerous skills needed for problem-solving and decision-making and for analysis of scientific inquiry and research-based knowledge development.
- Caring/relationship skills – This includes humanistic skills related to promoting patient-focused interests and concerns, sensitivity to cultural and ethnic beliefs and preferences, patient advocacy, social justice, and interpersonal behaviors that demonstrate care for patients and families.
- Teaching skills – This includes the ability to transmit information to instruct patients and staff about health and well-being.
- Management skills – This includes such skills as time management, resource management, activity implementation, budget creation, delegation and supervision, and collaboration across disciplines.
- Leadership skills – This includes activities that promote staff cooperation, morale, assertiveness, and risk-taking and promote creative planning for change and implementation of new policies and protocols.
- Knowledge integration skills – This includes using factual information, prior-learned knowledge, and basic principles to support decisions and actions and integrating best practices from nursing and other disciplines (Lewburg, 2005).

Research in the Evaluation Process

Case management provides nurses an opportunity to conduct research and to quantify the case management model. Research is the formal process for conducting analysis using the scientific method, which utilizes numerous problem-solving steps. These steps include problem identification hypothesis formation, observation, analysis, and conclusion. Research is either one of two categories: basic research or applied research. With basic research, the goal is to obtain knowledge. With applied research, the goal is to seek to apply the research knowledge to everyday situations (Cohen & Cesta, 2005).

With nursing research, the steps include assessment, diagnosis, outcome identification, planning, implementation, and evaluation. With case management analysis, the methodology takes many forms and encompasses different elements. Case management research can be evaluation research, an experiment, or a quasi-experiment. Data is gathered and analyzed to evaluate the effects of some form of change or a project. With this type of research, it is difficult to develop a classic experimental design. Factors that are controlled include severity of illness, age, gender, and concurrent problems (Cohen & Cesta, 2005).

Case Recording, Documentation, and Coding

Diagnostic-Related Group (DRG) Assignment

Assignment of a diagnostic-related group (DRG) is based on medical record documentation. This record must be complete, timely, thorough, legible, proper, and comprehensive to provide the proper information. This documentation is necessary because reimbursement is contingent on the diagnoses, diagnostic procedures, and surgical procedures. DRG assignment requires a principal diagnosis, secondary diagnosis, surgical procedures, comorbidities, complications, age, and discharge status (Cesta, 2005).

Medical Records Coding

The hospital coding staff assigns one DRG to each medical record for the hospital stay. This is based on the information documented by physicians, nurses, and other healthcare providers. Coders obtain information on the principal diagnosis, secondary diagnoses (one to eight), and the procedures (one to six), which are then assigned to the appropriate DRG. Documentation of comorbidities and complications is important for reimbursement. For many patients, DRG relative weight is doubled with the addition of a comorbidity/complication (CC) designation. Comorbidity is a preexisting condition that prolongs the length of stay by at least one day in 75% of cases. A complication is a condition that occurs during the hospital stay that increases the length of stay by at least one day in 75% of cases (Cesta, 2005).

Medical Record Documentation

Healthcare providers must document in the medical record for several reasons. Documentation is a way of communicating between members of the interdisciplinary team. Also, it provides supportive data for reimbursement; education; research; and legal protection to patients, healthcare providers, and healthcare facilities. Additionally, documentation is a mechanism for evaluating adequacy of patient care and medical necessity (Cesta, 2005).

There are numerous regulatory organizations that provide standards regarding medical record documentation. Medicare's Conditions of Participation specifies that medical records must be written accurately, be properly filed and retained, be completed promptly, and be accessible. Also, the final diagnosis must be documented within 30 days of discharge from the healthcare facility. The Joint Commission requires that the medical record contain sufficient documentation to support the diagnosis, justify treatment, and promote continuity among healthcare providers. All information and data is used by hospital coders for the selection of ICD-9 codes for reimbursement under the DRG system (Cesta, 2005).

The Coding Process

Hospital and clinical coders are trained professionals with knowledge of the ICD-9 coding system. These professionals can identify necessary billing codes in the patient's medical record. Each DRG has many ICD-9 codes that represent clinical conditions, designate diagnoses, and label procedures. Physician documentation is significant for accurate coding, and the provider and coding professional must work together to achieve accurate and complete documentation. Coded data is used to:

- Reimburse healthcare providers and organizations
- Expand the body of medical knowledge through research and education
- Improve the effectiveness and quality of patient care
- Assist in decision-making regarding healthcare delivery systems, policies, funding, and service expansion
- Monitor resource utilization
- Provide comparative data to consumers
- Facilitate the monitoring of fraud and abuse (Cesta, 2005)

Quality and Performance Improvement Concepts

Two significant components of the case manager's job are quality improvement and performance improvement. Both of these processes are necessary to maintain accreditation with the Joint Commission. Risk management programs work closely with quality improvement and performance improvement programs for provision of safety checks, incident reports, infection control surveillance, outcomes management, and case management assessments.

Quality Improvement

Quality improvement (QI) is a process mandated by accreditation organizations such as the Joint Commission. Often referred to as quality management (QM), QI is a means of improving various aspects of quality care such as policies and procedures, job descriptions, credentialing of professional staff, performance evaluations, educational programs, and continual monitoring activities. The Joint Commission also mandates evidence of performance management (PM) efforts. The continuous quality improvement (CQI) concept is related to the QI and risk management (RM) processes. QI and PM both involve the provision of excellent patient care (that is monitored and documented) through patient safety and quality of care, and both of these processes emphasize a proactive approach to quality service (Powell & Tahan, 2010).

Performance Improvement

Performance improvement (PI) involves the four-step process of design, improvement, measurement, and control. With the design step, the healthcare facility designs new functions or modifies existing ones and creates new services based on the vision and mission of the organization, the expectations of the patients and families, the identified concerns, and the latest information regarding the focus of improvement. The improvement step involves implementation of strategic changes and the desired outcomes. With the measurement step, the facility evaluates the effectiveness of the designed (or redesigned) process to find opportunities for further improvement or modification. The control step involves implementation of specific strategies to maintain the improvement of the process (Powell & Tahan, 2010).

Quality Assurance

Quality assurance cannot "assure" that maloccurrences do not happen, but through QI and PI measures, the risk manager can initiate the appropriate action to minimize the inevitable consequences. RM programs work closely with QI and PI programs for provision of safety checks, incident reports, infection control surveillance, outcomes management, and case management assessments. RM and QI are related programs with similar objectives. The case manager can conduct chart reviews to discover and expose potential problems in services or care (Powell & Tahan, 2010).

Risk Management

Traditional risk management (RM) focuses on identifying potential risk areas and interventions that will improve patient safety while preventing adverse events and unfortunate incidents. Risk-mitigated programs were developed to avoid the reactive nature of risk management activities. They allow the organization to proactively identify risks or failures and to implement interventions that will prevent these from occurring. Typical risk-mitigation activities include:

- Falls assessment programs
- Injury reduction programs
- Pressure ulcer prevention programs
- Infection control surveillance
- Failure mode analysis
- Prevention of deep vein thrombosis
- Daily review of patient flow activities (Powell & Tahan, 2010)

Outcomes Management

The four key functions of a case manager are assessment, planning, facilitation, and advocacy. Outcome measures in case management should demonstrate two key points: (1) the case manager has four key functions and (2) effective performance of these four functions positively impacts outcomes (Aliotta, 2005).

Outcomes are the consequences from received care or from omitted care. Poor outcomes often lead to policy and procedure changes, job description changes, and additional staff training and education. Outcomes management is a process that utilizes outcomes research to influence practice and involves the delivery of evidence-based care. With outcomes management, the case manager assesses and measures performance based on specific quality indicators at certain points in time. Also, he/she must monitor and evaluate performance using the same outcomes over time at specific intervals. This is called the longitudinal approach. Case managers also analyze and interpret results to find issues or concerns that must be addressed and take necessary actions to improve quality and performance (Powell & Tahan, 2010).

Case management combined with outcomes management improves patient care safety and quality and implementation of evidence-based standards, treatments, and protocols. Additionally, these combined efforts allow for a systematic evaluation of performance. Healthcare facilities report performance based on certain outcome indicators using a report card or score card. These reports communicate the contribution of case management to improved outcomes (Powell & Tahan, 2010).

Outcome Indicators

- Cost – Length of stay, cost per case, cost per day, and cost per service
- Utilization – Average number of laboratory tests or diagnostic tests per case
- Transitional planning – Discharge delays and readmissions within one week
- Clinical – Mortality rates, morbidity rates, and pain management
- Satisfaction – Comfort, well-being, and level of independence
- Variance – Systems-related, community-related, and patient-related (Powell & Tahan, 2010)

Quality of Life Indicators

Quality of life (QOL) is an outcome measure that documents the effectiveness of clinical interventions such as surgery, drug therapy, and treatments. QOL evaluates the patient's perception of his/her health, general sense of well-being, and satisfaction with life. These findings provide insight about the strengths and weaknesses of diagnostic, laboratory, and treatment therapies. Non-biomedical components that can be evaluated with QOL data are beliefs, values, coping abilities, social networks, spiritual status, vocational status, insurance policies, communication systems, and transportation (Nold, 2005).

Categories of QOL Indicators

Categories of QOL are also referred to as domains. One single overall QOL score may not reflect the differences in these categories. Also, one category can reflect decreased outcomes, whereas another can show improved outcomes. The categories are:

- Physical functioning – Limitations related to physical disabilities or issues
- Psychological functioning – Limitations related to emotional problems
- Social functioning – Limitations related to lack of social interaction
- Economic resources – Access to care and healthcare costs
- General well-being – General health perceptions (Nold, 2005)

QOL Instruments

Numerous tools are being used to assess health status and quality of life. Researchers use general non-disease-specific, disease-specific, population-specific, problem-specific, function-specific, and psychologically specific tools. These generic measures may not evaluate detailed aspects of functions and/or symptoms. The choice of measure is determined by the purpose and needs of the population and provider. QOL is often considered the gap between a patient's expectations and his/her actual achievements. Case managers can use QOL indicators to predict outcomes for patients and to identify patients with needs, meet those needs, and advise providers of system improvements (Nold, 2005).

Conflict Resolution

A case manager must possess certain leadership skills to serve in this position. Conflict management is a significant skill for case managers and other nurse leaders. Conflict can be within one's self (intrapersonal), between the self and another person (interpersonal), among members of a particular group (intragroup), or among members of two or more groups (intergroup). Competitive conflict occurs when the desired outcome is to overcome one's opponent. Conflict management occupies a substantial percentage of the case manager's time (Rundio & Wilson, 2010).

Conflict is a disagreement through which the involved parties perceive a threat to their interests, concerns, and/or needs. Workplace conflicts in the healthcare environment often involve complex relationships that are based on emotion. When a conflict involves substantive, psychological, or procedural dimensions, participants often respond on the basis of their perceptions of a particular situation. This perception is often filled with thoughts and emotions that guide the individual to a solution. Two important elements of conflict resolution that a case manager must be familiar with include understanding the types of conflicts that are commonly encountered and identifying effective strategies to manage these conflicts (Johansen, 2012).

Strategies for Conflict Resolution

- Focus on goals rather than on personalities – This involves careful consideration of the objectives that led to the conflict.
- Meet the needs of both parties equally (if possible)
- Build consensus (among all parties)
- Engage in dialogue – Case managers should engage in dialogue that addresses conflict and in conflict management behavior to create a healthy work environment.
- Coach and educate healthcare providers and nurses – This can be accomplished through role-playing exercises, staff meetings, educational videos, and effective communication.
- Identify potential conflicts – Conflicts are an inevitable part of the healthcare work environment. Case managers should develop procedures and processes

for identification of potential common conflicts (Johansen, 2012; Rundio & Wilson, 2010).

Ethical Conflict

Nurse case managers often try to prevent ethical conflict when it arises. Preventing and resolving ethical conflict facilitates early recognition of problematic situations and circumstances and facilitates timely communication among those associated with the decision-making process. When communication does not resolve a problem among the concerned parties, the case manager should consult or meet with the ethics committee. Successful mediation of ethical conflicts requires sensitivity to the problem and the ability to communicate factors that contributed to the conflict (Taylor, 2005).

Acuity Levels

Patient acuity is a concept that is significant to patient safety, and as acuity rises, more nurses are needed to provide adequate, safe care. Researchers and staffing experts have worked for more than 50 years developing methodologies to accurately indicate the number of nurses necessary for quality patient care. In the 1980s, patient classification systems (PCSs) were used to predict patient requirements related to personnel resources, quality, and costs. However, PCSs have many limitations such as validity and reliability issues, lack of credibility among staff and administrators, and complex and time-consuming preparation requirements (Jennings, 2013).

According to a literature review conducted by Jennings (2013), there is little empirical evidence concerning the relationship between acuity and patient safety, making the practice implications of most existing studies limited. Some studies show that there is a positive relationship between acuity and adult mortality, but for acuity and neonatal mortality rates, finds were more equivocal. Some researchers suggested that mortality is partially due to an excess workload. In many studies, acuity was found to be a significant predictor of various self-care measures such as symptom management.

Severity of Illness

Severity of illness (SI) represents a set of criteria, which are measurable and objective clinical indicators of a patient's condition. SI indicates how sick the patient is, what level of care is appropriate, and what treatments and services are necessary. The information is gathered from a patient assessment, and the time of symptoms' onset criterion is used as part of the definition. SI criteria include:

A. <u>Acute/sudden onset</u> – Within 24 hours
B. <u>Recent onset</u> – Within one week
C. <u>New onset</u> – Greater than one week
D. <u>Newly discovered</u> – New findings found during this illness episode (Powell & Tahan, 2010)

Examples

- Oral temperature of 104° Fahrenheit
- Sustained pulse greater than 100 bpm
- Respiratory rate greater than 26 with pulse oximeter less than 85% on room air
- Systolic blood pressure greater than 250 or less than 80 mmHg
- Diastolic blood pressure greater than 120 or less than 40 mmHg

Intensity of Service

Intensity of service (IS) represents a set of criteria, which define the diagnostic and therapeutic services for each category of severity of illness (SI). IS indicates what is being done for the patient, what level of care is being given, and what resources the patient needs. When IS criteria are preceded by an asterisk, this denotes that these criteria reflect a treatment that can be accomplished at a non-acute level of care. Level of care received by a patient must match the patient's severity of illness. IS involves the outcome used to ascertain whether the patient is receiving an adequate level of care (Powell & Tahan, 2010).

Discharge Screens

Discharge screens are parameters that are objective, functional, and indicate readiness and stability for discharge or transfer to another care level. These screens indicate whether the patient is clinically ready for discharge or transfer and whether the patient is stable enough for this process (Powell & Tahan, 2010).

Screening related to discharge planning is emphasized in Medicare's Conditions of Participation. These conditions maintain that the discharge plan be in writing and identify all patients likely to suffer adverse health consequences upon discharge. This implies that the case manager identify the subset of patients whose discharge plans are not routine and could include multifaceted, complex post-hospital care needs. A discharge screen with a cut-point score that suggests a course of action can function as a clinical prediction rule (Holland, Leibson, Pankratz et al., 2006).

The most frequently used discharge tools include the Hospital Admission Risk Profile (HARP), the Probability of ReAdmission (PRA), and the Blaylock Risk Assessment Screen Score (BRASS). The HARP was developed to predict a decline in function, whereas the PRA was created to predict hospital readmission, which is an outcome associated with poor discharge planning Also, the BRASS was developed to identify elderly hospitalized patients at risk for longer lengths of stay and more frequent admissions (Holland, Leibson, Pankratz et al., 2006).

InterQual's Intensity of Service Criteria

InterQual's review process of IS criteria involve four types of review: preadmission, admission, subsequent, and discharge reviews. Preadmission review is initiated before patient admission to the healthcare facility. The reviewer determines which diagnostic and therapeutic services and modalities match the patient's care level. The admission review is usually the initial chart review, done within 24 hours of admission. Subsequent reviews are done throughout the hospitalization, typically every three days. However, the frequency is often determined by the patient's care level and the SI. The discharge review is initiated when the patient is ready for discharge or transfer, and it involves documentation of discharge planning (Powell & Tahan, 2010).

Examples

- IV insulin
- Ventilator assistance
- Initial tracheostomy care
- IV antibiotics, antifungals, antidiuretics, or steroids
- IV or intramuscular (IM) analgesics (at least four in a 24-hour period)

Caseload Calculation

Caseload calculation includes the case mix index, caseload matrix, and hospital payment. The case manager is often responsible for determining caseload calculation.

Major Diagnostic Categories

Major diagnostic categories (MDCs) are formed by dividing all possible principal diagnoses from ICD-9 into 25 exclusive diagnosis areas. The MDC codes are similar to DRG codes, and they are primarily an administrative data element unique to the U.S. healthcare reimbursement system. The diagnosis of each MDC corresponds to a single body system or etiology, which is associated with a specific medical specialty. DRGs are separated into major diagnostic categories. The number of DRGs in each MDC ranges from 1 to 20, or more. MDCs are grouped according to anatomical and pathophysiological sections and how patients should be clinically managed. Also, MDCs are categorized as either medical or surgical (Cesta, 2005).

List of Major Diagnostic Categories

- 0 – Pre-MDC
- 1 – Nervous System
- 2 – Eye
- 3 – Ear, Nose, Mouth, and Throat
- 4 – Respiratory System
- 5 – Circulatory System
- 6 – Digestive System
- 7 – Hepatobiliary System and Pancreas
- 8 – Musculoskeletal System and Connective Tissue
- 9 – Skin, Subcutaneous Tissue, and Breast

- 10 – Endocrine, Nutritional, and Metabolic Systems
- 11 – Kidney and Urinary Tract
- 12 – Male Reproductive System
- 13 – Female Reproductive System
- 14 – Pregnancy, Childbirth, and Puerperium
- 15 – Newborn and Other Neonates
- 16 – Blood and Immunological Disorders
- 17 – Myeloproliferative DDs
- 18 – Infectious and Parasitic DDs
- 19 – Mental Diseases and Disorders
- 20 – Alcohol/Drug Use or Induced Mental Disorders
- 21 – Injuries, Poison, and Toxic Effects of Drugs
- 22 – Burns
- 23 – Factors Influencing Health Status
- 24 – Multiple Significant Trauma
- 25 – Human Immunodeficiency Virus Infection

Case Mix Index (CMI)

With DRGs, patients are classified into groups by condition or illness. This is based on the primary and secondary diagnoses, procedures, patient needs, comorbidities, complexity of illness, and patient age. Each DRG has a relative average value assigned to it, and this value indicates the amount of resources necessary to care for patients in that group. This relative average value is called the case mix index (CMI). The CMI is the sum of all DRG-related weights divided by the number of patients cared for during a specified period of time, typically one calendar year. With a high CMI, the case mix complexity of the hospital is also greater (Cesta, 2005).

Hospital CMI

The CMI of a hospital reflects the clinical complexity, diversity, and need for resources of a patient population in that healthcare facility. The CMI value of a hospital is used to adjust the average cost per patient (or cost per day per patient) relative to the adjusted average cost for other facilities. This is calculated by dividing the average cost per patient by the hospital's calculated CMI. The adjusted cost per patient reflects the reported charges for the types of DRGs treated in that calendar year. If a hospital has a CMI greater than 1.00, the organization's adjusted cost per patient per day will be lower. If the hospital has a CMI less than 1.00, these costs will be higher (Cesta, 2005).

Factors that Affect the Case Mix Index

Severity of illness and prognosis dictate the complexity and types of services provided, and the case mix influences hospital costs. Basically, the number of patients does not affect hospital costs as much as the types of patients and the use of resources. Case mix index values depend on:

A. Severity of illness
B. Need for intervention
C. Treatment difficulty
D. Presence of complications and/or comorbidities (Cesta, 2005)

Caseload Matrix

The caseload matrix is used in caseload calculation to identify variables in different settings that could affect caseload. The caseload matrix is a schematic chart with four major categories, which contain the elements known to affect caseload complexity and size. These elements are derived from several input streams including the diverse professional experience of case managers and social workers. Changes in one component of the chart can alter outcomes, elements, and functions in other categories. Elements of the caseload matrix that can affect caseload are:

- Business environment and market segment
- Regulatory and legal requirements
- Clinical practice setting
- Environmental factors
- Psychosocial factors
- CM outcomes
- Long-term outcomes (Cesta, 2005)

Initial Elements Impacting Caseload

Category one of the caseload matrix contains elements that describe the context and situation in which case management occurs. These context elements include: business environment, market segment, regulatory and legal requirements, clinical practice setting, individual case manager factors (such as skill levels), type of medical management services, and technology support. Case management practice is impacted by regulatory influences. These changes include alterations in regulations imposed by the Centers for Medicare and Medicaid (CMS) such as "Pay for Performance" and "Patient-Centered Medical Homes" (Case Management Society of America, 2008).

The practice setting also affects the case manager-to-patient ratio. The skill level of the case manager is an element for consideration in caseload determinations. An experienced case manager can negotiate difficult situations in less time and with greater efficiency and success than a less experienced case manager. Because of the development of a versatile set of skills, experienced case managers can manage a caseload with more complex cases and higher patient acuities than can less experienced case managers (Case Management Society of America, 2008).

Patient outcomes are both intermediate and long-term. With intermediate outcomes, numerous changes are evaluated with the caseload matrix such as alterations in the patient's health-related behaviors, adherence, environmental barriers, and those associated with safe and effective transition of care. Long-term outcomes pertain to the appropriate use of healthcare services, improved health status, cost effectiveness, and improved quality of life (Case Management Society of America, 2008).

Hospital Payment

Hospital payment is calculated by multiplying the relative weight with the facility's base rate. Each healthcare facility is assigned a base rate for reimbursement by CMS. This rate is determined by population served, geographic location, cost of living in the area, type of hospital (teaching, academic, or community), and types of services (Cesta, 2005).

Chapter 2: Principles of Practice

Accreditation Standards and Requirements

Accreditation of case management organizations is done to assist individual case managers in reaching the full extent of their practice ability. Accreditation also shows the quality of the program to purchasers of the program and to the public. The organizations that offer accreditation programs for case management programs include Commission on Accreditation of Rehabilitation Facilities (CARF), Utilization Review Accreditation Commission (URAC), Accreditation Commission for Health Care (ACHC), National Committee for Quality Assurance (NCQA), and the Joint Commission on Accreditation of Healthcare Organizations (JCAHO). The CARF standards are aimed toward medical rehabilitation case management, and the URAC standards apply more to payer-based programs (Boling & Severson, 2005).

Commission on Accreditation of Rehabilitation Facilities (CARF)

The leadership section of CARF addresses who is responsible for directing medical rehabilitation case management. This section outlines responsibilities for various areas of case management activity such as health, safety, ethics, fiscal management, and transportation. The information and outcomes management section addresses how the information is collected and the level of the program used to determine the case manager's outcomes and interventions. CARF has many case management accreditation programs related to the practice arena including:

- Initial and ongoing assessments
- Effective and efficient use of resources
- Knowledge and awareness of care options
- Individualized plans based on specific patient needs
- Predicted outcomes
- Regulatory, legislative, and financial implications (Boling & Severson, 2005)

Utilization Review Accreditation Commission (URAC)

URAC uses a modular approach to accreditation. They have 43 CORE standards that all organizations must meet for accreditation. These standards apply to case management organizations that provide on-site or telephone case management services along with privately or publicly funded benefit programs. Some of the CORE standards include:

- Organization structure
- Policies and procedures
- Information management
- Interdepartmental coordination
- Clinical oversight

- Regulatory compliance
- Communications
- Quality management
- Patient and family satisfaction (Boling & Severson, 2005)

The Accreditation Process

Accreditation is the cumulative review of the case management program structure and processes that are in place. This process reviews the documentation of policies and procedures and assesses how well the healthcare facility implements these policies and procedures. The accreditation process encompasses a review of documentation to assess the policies, procedures, and processes of the healthcare facility. An on-site evaluation is done to evaluate organizational function and compliance with guidelines. Accrediting entities address the following areas:

- Caseload size
- Case management qualifications
- Evaluation in the case management program
- Collection and analysis of data for cost, access, and confidentiality
- Outcome studies (Boling & Severson, 2005)

Ethics

Ethics in healthcare involve morals, choices, and the basic rights of free choice and autonomy. Ethical dilemmas often arise in situations where ethically correct courses of action are unclear. Case managers are faced with various ethical dilemmas such as withholding or withdrawing care. Ethically competent case managers are able to act in ways that protect the interests of their patients and mediate ethical conflicts whenever they occur (Banja, 2008).

Ethical Principles of Case Management

- Autonomy – An ethical principle that represents individual liberty, self-determination, personal inviolability, and anti-paternalism. An example is the patient's right to refuse case management services.
- Non-maleficence – An ethical principle that is fundamental to healthcare where the professional is obligated to "do no harm." An example of harming the patient would be when the case manager writes reports that bias the payer against the patient.
- Beneficence – An ethical principle that requires the professional to do as much good as he/she can. An example of this is a choice between returning to work versus receiving unemployment benefits.
- Justice – An ethical principle where the patient receives what he/she is owed and involves fair treatment. An example of this is when the case manager

believes the patient is noncompliant and cannot advocate for him/her (Banja, 2008).

Ethical Behavior Strategies

- <u>Form ethics committees and groups</u> – To address ethical conflicts and dilemmas as they occur, it is necessary for healthcare facilities to organize ethics committees and groups. These committees and groups are comprised of people who are known for professional expertise, for professional integrity, and for maintaining high ethical and legal standards.
- <u>Understand the types of ethical conflicts that can arise</u> – Clinical ethical conflicts are related to medical treatment (such as end-of-life matters), lack of patient/family understanding of medical treatment, and conflict regarding best treatment options. Organizational ethical conflicts are related to individuals of the healthcare facility and pertain to an organization's behaviors. Examples include denial of services, conflicts of interest, and allocation of resources.
- <u>Be able to justify an ethical act</u> – Case managers should be able to analyze the reasons for certain decisions and decide whether or not those reasons will withstand both public and professional scrutiny.
- <u>Be familiar with the Commission for Case Manager Certification's Code of Professional Conduct for Case Managers</u> – This is the ethical code of the profession, and case managers should review this code and standards regularly.

- Work within the case management scope of practice – This includes adherence to professional guidelines and job descriptions (Banja, 2008).

Code of Professional Conduct for Case Managers

First published in 1996, the Code of Professional Conduct for Case Managers requires case managers to adhere to five principles of professional conduct: (1) autonomy, (2) beneficence, (3) non-maleficence, (4) justice, and (5) veracity. Also, case managers must adhere to six standards of professional conduct:

1. Advocacy – This focuses on the role of the case manager as a patient advocate.
2. Professional responsibility – This involves the areas of practice, competence, representation of qualifications, use of CCM designation, conflict of interest, legal and benefit system requirements, and compliance proceedings.
3. Case manager and patient relationship – This focuses on description of services to patients, relationships with patients, termination of services or case closure, and objectivity.
4. Confidentiality, privacy, and record-keeping – This describes the role of the case manager in legal compliance, client identity, electronic recordings, disclosure, storage, disposal, and reporting.
5. Professional relationships – This addresses dual relationships, testimony, unprofessional behaviors, solicitation, advertising, and fees.
6. Research – This focuses on subject privacy and legal compliance issues (Powell & Tahan, 2010).

Healthcare and Disability-Related Legislation

In 1993, the Health Security Act was initiated. This reform package was created by a task force for the purpose of developing a comprehensive plan to provide universal healthcare for all Americans. The main element of the plan was to force employers to provide health insurance coverage for all their employees, which would be regulated by health maintenance organizations. In 1994, Congress ended two prospects for the legislation. Comprehensive healthcare reform in the U.S. was not enacted by Congress until the Patient Protection and Affordable Care Act in 2010 (Cohen & Cesta, 2005).

The Social Health Maintenance Organization (SHMO)

The social health maintenance organization (SHMO) is a national managed care demonstration program that provides and finances long-term care for the elderly. This program was approved by Congress in 1985, and it includes four nonprofit sites. This initiative uses case management and integrated healthcare service delivery at all sites, and it is recognized as one of the few national demonstration projects to adequately include acute and chronic care with existing funding resources through a capitated system (Cohen & Cesta, 2005).

Employee Retirement Income Security Act (ERISA)

The Employee Retirement Income Security Act (ERISA) of 1974 involves the regulation of pension plans. ERISA was enacted so that employers who hire employees in multistate locations are not bothered with multiple state laws. For case managers, those who work with employer health plans or self-funded plans must consider the other aspects of this law. This way, the benefit plan becomes the controlling document for established coverage, coordination of benefits, claims processing, appeals procedures, and all other rules governing beneficiaries (Muller, 2010).

ERISA presents many issues regarding litigation in healthcare. Case managers who work with patients under ERISA should request counsel with legal experts regarding various predicaments. In many cases, federal law supersedes state law, especially with the administration of the ERISA plan (Muller, 2010).

The Federal Workforce Flexibility Act of 2004

The Federal Workforce Flexibility Act of 2004 added many strategies that support human capital management. The underlying expectation for all of these changes is strategic capital management to ensure that all human resource activity directly contributes to achieving results (U.S. Office of Personnel Management, 2013).

Family and Medical Leave Act (FMLA)

The Family and Medical Leave Act (FMLA) entitles eligible employees of certain covered employers to take unpaid, job-protected leave for specified medical and family reasons with continuation of group health insurance coverage (U.S. Department of Labor, 2013).

Covered Employers

The FMLA applies only to certain employers. These include a:

A. Private-sector employer with 50 or more employees in 20 or more workweeks in the current or preceding calendar year including a successor or joint employer in interest to a covered employer
B. Public agency including local, state, or federal agencies, regardless of the number of employees
C. Public or private elementary or secondary school, regardless of the number of employees (U.S. Department of Labor, 2013)

Eligible Employees

An eligible employee is someone who:

- Works for a covered employer
- Has worked for the employer for at least 12 months
- Has at least 1,250 hours of service for the employer during that 12-month period
- Works at a location where the employer has at least 50 employees (U.S. Department of Labor, 2013)

Eligible Employee Benefits

Eligible employees are entitled to 12 workweeks of leave in a one-year period:

- For the birth of a child and to care for the newborn during this time frame
- To care for a child, spouse, or parent with a serious health condition
- To care for an adopted child or a child in newly placed foster care
- For a serious health condition that renders the employee unable to work
- For any qualifying exigency arising from the fact that the employee's spouse, son, daughter, or parent is a covered military member on "covered active duty" (U.S. Department of Labor, 2013)

Eligible employees are entitled to 26 workweeks of leave during a one-year period:

- To care for a covered service member with a serious injury or illness if the eligible employee is the service member's spouse, son, daughter, parent, or next-of-kin (U.S. Department of Labor, 2013)

Americans with Disabilities Act (ADA)

In 1990, the Americans with Disabilities Act (ADA) was signed into law. This law ensures that qualified individuals with disabilities enjoy the same employment opportunities as those without any physical or mental disability. According to the ADA, the term disability has three distinct definitions:

- A physical or mental impairment that substantially limits one or more major life activities
- A record of such impairment
- Being regarded as having such an impairment (U.S. Department of Justice, 2013)

Reasonable Accommodation

According to the Equal Employment Opportunity Commission (EEOC), reasonable accommodation means modifications:

A. To the job application process that allow a qualified individual with a disability to be considered for a certain position

B. To the work environment, circumstances, or manner under which the position is held

C. To allow a qualified person with a disability to perform the necessary work functions

D. To enable an employee with a disability to profit from the same privileges and benefits as those without disabilities (U.S. Department of Justice, 2013)

Fair Labor Standards Act (FLSA)

The Fair Labor Standards Act (FLSA) establishes minimum wage, record-keeping, overtime pay, and young employment standards for full-time and part-time workers in the private sector and in local, state, and federal governments. This law covers more than 85% of all non-supervisory employees. The FLSA includes certain regulations regarding waiting time; on-call time; preparatory and concluding activities; and attendance of meetings, lectures, training programs, and other employer-related functions. The U.S. Department of Labor's Wage and Hour Division regulates FLSA for local and state government employment; private employment; and federal employment in the U.S. Postal Service, Tennessee Valley Authority, Postal Rate Commission, and Library of Congress (U.S. Department of Labor, 2013).

Wage and Hour Laws

The three most common violations by employers involve compensation, record-keeping, and exemption status. Important legislation regarding these areas includes:

- FLSA Child Labor Provisions – The child labor provisions establish the basic minimum age for employment, which is 16 years. However, employment of 14- and 15-year-old youths is allowed for certain occupations and under specific guidelines.

- FLSA Amendments of 1989 – The U.S. Department of Labor's Wage and Hour Division implemented amendments to the FLSA that require employees lacking basic skills to receive additional remedial training in addition to their 40-hour workweek.

- Equal Pay Act of 1963 – The Equal Pay Act requires that men and women performing equal work receive equal pay. This act prohibits discrimination based on gender regarding compensation for work services (Rundio & Wilson, 2010).

Equal Employment Opportunity Commission (EEOC)

The EEOC enforces Title VII of the Civil Rights Act of 1964, the Age Discrimination in Employment Act (ADEA) of 1967, and the Rehabilitation Act of 1973. Equal employment laws involve various aspects of discrimination due to color, race, religion, age, national origin, sex, pregnancy, sexual orientation, and sexual harassment. The EEOC governs the law's interpretation and settles disputes regarding discrimination. This organization attempts to reach an agreement between the employee and employer through persuasion and conciliation. If an agreement is not reached, the EEOC can bring a civil action lawsuit against an employer on behalf of the person or persons claiming to be aggrieved (U.S. Equal Employment Opportunity Commission, 2013a).

Rehabilitation Act of 1973

The Rehabilitation Act of 1973 ensures that qualified individuals with handicaps are not excluded from participation in various programs and activities or denied benefits from the employer. This regulation prohibits the discrimination against an employee with a disability who is otherwise qualified. A qualified handicapped person is someone who can perform the main functions of the job with reasonable accommodations (U.S. Equal Employment Opportunity Commission, 2013b).

Occupational Safety and Health Administration (OSHA)

The Occupational Safety and Health Administration (OSHA) governs any employer who operates or engages in a business that affects commerce. This administration requires employers to provide each employee a place of work that is free from recognized hazards that have or can result in serious physical harm or death (OSHA, 2013a). The Occupational Safety and Health Act of 1970 is broadly written federal legislation, modeled after the California OSHA programs. Since its inception, the law has been amended several times (OSHA, 2013b).

OSHA is authorized to conduct workplace inspection on each business covered by the OSH Act. The U.S. Department of Labor governs OSHA and allows it to conduct an inspection at the request of an employer or in response to an employee complaint. The reports that are considered top priority are those that indicate imminent dangers, fatalities, or accidents that send three or more workers to the hospital. The Site-Specific Targeting Program focuses on employers who report increased illness rates or high injury percentages. OSHA also emphasizes programs that focus on hazardous work such as work with mechanical power press equipment or trenching (Rundio & Wilson, 2010).

Record-Keeping

To verify compliance with the OSH Act, OSHA requires employers to keep certain records. OSHA supplies certain forms to employers through the OSHA website. Employers with 11 or more employees must keep records of work-related illnesses and injuries. This encompasses around 1.5 million companies and organizations, or 20% of the establishments covered by OSHA. Workplaces that are exempt from record-keeping include low-hazard industries such as finance, retail, insurance, real estate, and service (OSHA, 2013c).

OSHA Cooperative Plans

Five types of cooperative plans that increase workplace safety are offered by OSHA. These are:

- VPP – A reduction of lost workdays increases worker protection, decreases business costs, improves employee morale, and enhances productivity. Worksite Voluntary Protection Programs (VPP) document lost workday cases of around 70%, which are lower than their industry averages. These results were verified by OSHA.

- Alliance Program – The Alliance Program works in conjunction with several other organizations that are involved with workplace health and safety including unions, employers, trade groups, professional organizations, and education institutions.

- OSPP – The Strategic Partnership Program (OSPP) is for employers with special interest and experience in job safety and health who also have a commitment to improving workplace safety.

- Challenge Program – OSHA Challenge Program provides interested employers and employees the opportunity to gain assistance in improving their health and safety management systems. This program uses a three-stage process to prevent injuries, illness, and fatalities.

- SHARP – Safety and Health Achievement Recognition Program (SHARP) offers employers that have a full on-site consultation visit who meet certain requirements to be recognized for exemplary management systems. Worksites that receive the SHARP recognition are exempt from OSHA inspections during the valid inspection period (OSHA, 2013d).

Workers' Compensation

With the Workers' Compensation law, an employee who becomes ill or who is injured on the job or from a condition caused by the worksite is compensated for that incident. This includes reimbursement for hospital costs and medical care. Workers' compensation acts are state statutes, which establish liability of employers for injuries or illnesses to or of workers on the job due to the employment. Workers' compensation entails absolute liability for medical coverage, costs of rehabilitation, a percentage of wages or salary, and payment for permanent injury (Rundio & Wilson, 2010).

Legal and Regulatory Requirements

The Legal System

Understanding the law is difficult for those without the proper education. Case managers must be aware of various legal terms and understand state and federal laws. The legal system is divided into two categories: civil and criminal law. Civil law applies to the private rights of a person, whereas criminal law deals with crimes and the prosecution of those who commit them. A tort is a civil wrong, whereas a crime is a public wrong. Legal issues that affect case management involve healthcare provider licensure, quality care services, and various rules and regulations (Muller, 2008).

Intentional Torts

Intentional torts include assault, battery, trespass, and false imprisonment. These terms also exist in criminal law, but they are defined by statute when applicable. Each intentional tort is a direct insult to a person's physical integrity and right to property. Informed consent is an example of a knowing and voluntary waiver of personal rights in the healthcare setting. Without this document, there is no waiver of rights, and the healthcare provider can be liable for assault, battery, or false imprisonment (Muller, 2008).

Professional Negligence and Malpractice

With legal malpractice, there are four elements that apply: duty, breach, cause, and harm. All of these elements must be proven for a lawsuit to be successful. Negligence is often referred to as simple negligence as compared to professional negligence and malpractice. The concept of negligence is based on the assumption that there is a general standard of human behavior. Licensure in the healthcare profession assures the public that the person has the necessary qualifications to perform his/her job. Nurse practice acts provide broad statements defining the practice of nursing and delineating the requirements for licensure. The first level of scrutiny of a case manager's liability is his/her underlying profession (Muller, 2008).

Liability Exposure for Case Managers

Case management is required by law in many circumstances and in various states in the U.S. Case management services are provided through a contractual relationship, with many patients having services through employment or the workers' compensation system. Case managers must be aware of various laws regarding case management practice. In 1995, a New Jersey Supreme Court held an HMO partially liable for the malpractice of a physician who was hired by that organization as an independent contractor. Therefore, it is possible that a case manager who provides an HMO case management services could be held liable for various acts and actions. This concept is called joint liability (Muller, 2008).

Risk Management

Risk management (RM) focuses on the identification of potential risk areas and on interventions that will improve patient safety and prevent adverse events or losses before they occur. In many healthcare organizations, the RM team is called in after an unfortunate incident has occurred. The team must then attempt to control and minimize losses through legal processes and public relation efforts (Powell & Tahan, 2010).

RM and QI Similarities

- Both attempt to identify risk patterns and avoid adverse patient outcomes.
- Both involve monitoring trends to identify risk problems or patterns.
- Both require cooperation from the multidisciplinary team.
- Both use similar tools and techniques to identify and resolve problematic issues.
- Both require complete and clear documentation (Powell & Tahan, 2010).

RM and QI Differences

A. RM is concerned with care from a financial and legal perspective, minimizing the costs of liability, whereas QI is concerned with patient care issues and outcomes.
B. RM investigates patient and visitor safety, environment, and exposures, whereas QI investigates patient-care-focused issues such as optimal quality of care and adherence to professional standards.
C. RM attempts to decrease adverse patient outcomes, whereas QI aims to increase quality patient outcomes.
D. RM focuses on loss prevention, whereas QI assists with the enhancement of care and associated quality outcomes (Powell & Tahan, 2010).

Adverse Patient Outcomes

An adverse patient outcome (APO) is any adverse patient occurrence that should not happen under natural circumstances with the patient's disease process or as the end-result of a medical and/or surgical procedure. Many healthcare facilities have a severity coding system for APOs. These include levels I, II, and III (Powell & Tahan, 2010).

- Level I – There is an identified quality problem with minimal potential for adverse effects on the patient. An example is a patient discharged with mild hematuria without a follow-up plan. Also included in this level are certain events that are predictable within an expected standard of care such as urinary retention after a total hysterectomy.

- Level II – There is an identified quality problem with significant potential for adverse effects on the patient. An example is when the wrong intravenous medication is given, but the infusion was stopped before any harm occurred.

- Level III – There is an identified quality problem with significant deviation from acceptable levels of care, and it results in injury or harm to the patient. An example is the loss of a limb or death related to poor medical/nursing care (Powell & Tahan, 2010).

Root Cause Analysis

The process for identifying, investigating, reporting, and correcting APOs is called root cause analysis (RCA). This process involves a multidisciplinary team that includes risk managers, quality improvement managers, and personnel from the patient safety department. Some APOs must be reported to accreditation agencies or the state's Department of Health. Most RCA processes include a study of the environment where the APO occurred; identification of the personnel, equipment, and actions that were associated with the event; verification of the involved variables; and frequency-of-causes ranking (Powell & Tahan, 2010).

Incident Report

An incident is an error, accident, or the discovery of a hazardous condition that is not consistent with quality standards of care or practice. A potentially compensable event is one that could result in litigation. Variances are deviations from expected and acceptable care. The incident report is a communication tool used to record all of these things. This document is used by RM personnel to assess for potential liabilities, document existing problems, and show the need for policy and procedure revision. State law specifies whether the incident report can be used in court (Powell & Tahan, 2010).

CMS Core Measures

Core measures are set by the Centers for Medicare & Medicaid Services (CMS). These criteria are national, standardized performance measurements used to improve the quality of care. The CMS system is often referred to as National Quality Measures. The core measures include:

- Eight measures related to myocardial infarction care
- Four measures related to heart failure care
- Seven measures related to pneumonia care
- Five measures related to surgical infection prevention
- Three measures related to asthma care for children (Powell & Tahan, 2010)

Standards of Practice

The CMSA specifies standards of practice for case managers. These standards are considered "performance indicators," and are essential elements in case management practice, education, and training. The educational components include patient identification and selection for services, problem identification, planning, monitoring, evaluating, and outcomes. The performance indicators include quality care, qualifications for case managers, collaboration with healthcare providers and patients, and several legal and ethical considerations (Stanton & Tahan, 2008).

CMSA Standards of Practice also address resource management and provide set guidelines that are measurable for each of the performance indicators. Additionally, the standards specify certification and educational qualifications for case managers such as professional licensure, a minimum of two years of experience, appropriate continuing education, and certification (Stanton & Tahan, 2008).

CMSA Standards of Practice for Case Management

- Standard A: Patient Selection Process for Case Management – The case manager should identify and select clients who can most benefit from case management services available in a particular practice setting.

- Standard B: Patient Assessment – The case manager should complete a health and psychosocial assessment, considering the cultural and linguistic needs of each client.

- Standard C: Problem/Opportunity Identification – The case manager should identify problems or opportunities that would benefit from case management intervention.

- Standard D: Planning –The case manager should identify immediate, short-term, long-term, and ongoing needs and should develop appropriate and necessary case management strategies and goals to address those needs.

- Standard E: Monitoring – The case manager should employ ongoing assessment and documentation to measure the client's response to the plan of care.

- Standard F: Outcomes – The case manager should maximize the client's health, wellness, safety, adaptation, and self-care through quality case management, client satisfaction, and cost-efficiency.

- Standard G: Termination of Case Management Services – The case manager should appropriately terminate case management services based upon CMSA Standards of Practice for Case Management.

- Standard H: Facilitation, Coordination, and Collaboration – The case manager should facilitate coordination, communication, and collaboration with the client and other stakeholders to achieve goals and maximize positive client outcomes.

- Standard I: Qualifications for Case Management – Case managers should maintain competence in their areas of practice by having ONE of the following:
    a) An individual must hold a current, active, and unrestricted licensure or certification in a health or human services discipline that allows the professional to conduct an assessment independently as permitted within the scope of practice of the discipline.

    b) In the case of an individual in a state that does not require licensure or certification, the individual must have a baccalaureate or graduate degree in social work or another health or human services field that promotes the physical, psychosocial, and/or vocational well-being of the persons being served. The degree must be from an institution that is fully accredited by a nationally recognized educational accreditation organization, and the individual must have completed a supervised field experience in case management, health, or behavioral health as part of the degree.

- Standard J: Legal – The case manager should adhere to applicable local, state, and federal laws and employer policies governing all aspects of case management practice including client privacy and confidentiality rights. It is the responsibility of the case manager to work within the scope of his/her licensure.
    o NOTE: In the event that employer policies or the policies of other entities conflict with applicable legal requirements, the case manager should understand which laws prevail. In these cases, case managers should seek clarification of any questions or concerns from an appropriate, reliable, and expert resource such as an employer, government agency, or legal counsel.

    o Standard 1: Confidentiality and Client Privacy – The case manager should adhere to applicable local, state, and federal laws and employer policies governing the client, client privacy, and confidentiality rights and should act in a manner consistent with the client's best interest.

    o Standard 2: Consent for Case Management Services – The case manager should obtain appropriate and informed client consent before case management services are implemented.

- Standard K: Ethics – Case managers should behave and practice ethically, adhering to the tenets of the code of ethics that govern his/her professional credentials (nursing, social work, rehabilitation counseling, etc.).

- Standard L: Advocacy – The case manager should advocate for the client at the service-delivery, benefits-administration, and policy-making levels.
- Standard M: Cultural Competency – The case manager should be aware of, and responsive to, cultural and demographic diversity of the population and specific client profiles.

- Standard N: Resource Management and Stewardship – The case manager should integrate factors related to quality, safety, access, and cost-effectiveness in assessing, monitoring, and evaluating resources for the client's care.

- Standard O: Research and Research Utilization – The case manager should maintain familiarity with current research findings and be able to apply them, as appropriate, in his/her practice (Case Management Society of America, 2010).

Quality Indicators

Quality indicators are specific and measurable guides for evaluating and monitoring significant aspects of patient care. These indicators are usually written to improve patient care in various hospital settings, and each service has its own quality indicators. These indicators also include core measures and case management outcome indicators. Many healthcare facilities group all quality indicators together, whether or not they relate to case management (Powell & Tahan, 2010).

Outcome Measure Indicators

Category	Outcome Measures
Clinical	Morbidity rates
	Complication rates
	Mortality rates
Cost	Length of stay
	Cost per day
	Cost per case
Utilization	Denial rate
	Appeals conversion rate
	Surgical delays

Transitional Planning	Return to operating room
	Return to intensive care unit
	Readmission within 1 week of discharge
Satisfaction	Patient experience
	State of well-being
	Comfort
Variance	System-related Community-related
	Practitioner-related (Powell & Tahan, 2010)

Core Measure Indicators

Disease Category	*Core Measures*
Acute myocardial infarction	Aspirin on arrival
	LDL cholesterol assessment
	Adult smoking cessation counseling
Heart failure	Evaluation for LV systolic function
	ACE inhibitor for LV systolic dysfunction
	Adult smoking cessation counseling
Pneumonia	Oxygenation assessment
	Pneumococcal vaccination
	Initial antibiotic within 4 hours of arrival
Pediatric asthma	Immediate relievers
	Systemic corticosteroids
	Home management plan of care
Surgical infection prevention	Prophylactic antibiotic within 1 hour before
	Appropriate hair removal

	Appropriate thromboembolism prophylaxis (U.S. Department of Health and Human Services, 2013)

Confidentiality and HIPAA

The Health Insurance Portability & Accountability Act (HIPAA) of 1996 provides healthcare coverage continuity, simplifies administrative functions within the healthcare industry, and ensures greater accountability. The HIPAA Privacy Rule provides federal protection for individually identifiable healthcare information held by covered facilities and their business associates. It also gives patients many rights concerning that information and permits the disclosure of information unless specified by the legislation. The Security Rule of HIPAA specifies a series of physical, administrative, and technical safeguards for facilities and their business associates to use for the purpose of confidentiality, availability, and integrity of electronic protected healthcare information (Muller, 2008).

Medical records can legally be used for auditing, billing, quality assurance procedures, utilization review, and research. If the record is used for any of these reasons, or when the patient files a lawsuit based on his/her medical condition, HIPAA privacy protections are waived by the patient to allow permitted uses of the necessary medical record information. The case manager must ensure that the patient has been informed of his/her HIPAA rights and responsibilities, document this with a signed form, and take necessary steps to make sure that the patient's wishes are honored (Muller, 2008).

Chapter 3: Psychosocial Aspects

The psychological part of the case management assessment process is where the case manager evaluates and treats the entire family unit as the patient. In many social cultures, the extended family is a primary social unit with the parents acting as the decision-makers instead of the patient. There is not always a relationship between the severity of illness and psychological functioning, so the patient's response to the event or illness must be evaluated along with the family's adjustment to it (Powell & Tahan, 2010).

Abuse and Neglect

Child abuse has many variations and exists in all ethnic and socioeconomic groups. Child abuse reporting is mandatory, and if a classic case is not reported, healthcare providers who are involved in the child's care can be charged criminally and found negligent. Child abuse includes non-accidental injuries, exploitation, and sexual abuse. Elder abuse has many of the same characteristics as child abuse. This event is also covered under the mandatory reporting requirements. Adult abuse can take many forms including neglect, exploitation of property, sexual assault, medical neglect, psychological abuse, and unreasonable confinement. With elder abuse, the adult is vulnerable, incapacitated, and/or cannot defend himself/herself (Muller, 2010).

Domestic violence is a problem many emergency department healthcare workers encounter. Case managers must be sensitive to the patient's symptoms and injuries, recognizing that many victims of domestic violence remain silent. Many healthcare organizations report that domestic abuse is a health problem of epidemic proportion. Case managers are responsible for dealing with domestic violence victims regarding area resources, safe houses, and healthcare issues (Muller, 2010).

Psychological abuse involves intimidation measures and threats. This occurs when caregivers make frequent threats to hit the person and/or use intimidation with a weapon when the person does not cooperate. Psychological abuse makes the patient feel anxious and terrified. Neglect is the failure to provide basic needs, and it can be intentional (active) or unintentional (inactive). Financial abuse includes stealing, fraud, and forcing people to sign away property. Physical abuse involves various types of assaults such as biting, hitting, pulling hair, kicking, pushing, and shoving (Rittenmeyer, 2010).

An indication of financial abuse is the disappearance of items from the home. Family, caregivers, and friends often take one or two items at time, assuming that the person will not notice. Other forms of financial abuse include forcing a patient to sign over property, outright stealing of property, persuading patients to turn over possessions, using stolen credit cards, emptying bank accounts, convincing the person to invest money in a fraudulent scheme, and taking money for home renovations that do not get completed (Rittenmeyer, 2010).

Multicultural Issues and Health Behavior

Evaluation of patients should involve an assessment of their value systems, traditions, and beliefs. Aspects of cultural and religious diversity include:

- Gestures – In many cultures, non-verbal body language is a communication method such as nods, smiles, frowns, shoulder-shrugging, and turning away from the other person.

- Language barriers – This can lead to misunderstandings, which can alter or hinder the case management relationship.

- Traditions, taboos, and differences – There are many cultural-related traditions and taboos. What is right for one culture may be different for another. Some people do not approve of eye contact, feeling that it is impolite and that it "robs them of their spirit." Many cultures frown upon casual touching. Silence is necessary for some cultures, but uncomfortable for others.

- Religious and spiritual beliefs – For some cultures, the spiritual belief system is a major source of strength. There are numerous religious and dietary practices to consider. Jehovah's Witness members do not believe in blood transfusions, which can alter the treatment plan and create ethical concerns.

- Health and illness – When it comes to beliefs about health, culture is a major contributing factor. In many non-Western cultures, people believe that illness comes from natural or unnatural causes. The natural causes that some believe contribute to health problems include heat, cold, dampness, and wind. Therefore, the person may not think that medicines would affect his/her health status. Unnatural causes that are thought to contribute to illness include spirits, supernatural forces, and deities (Powell & Tahan, 2010).

Behavioral Health and Psychiatric Disability Concepts

Behavioral health case management is a strategy for healthcare delivery to all persons with mental health disorders, involving the aspects of high-cost, high-volume, and high-risk populations. The major cost of behavioral healthcare is multiple episodes of psychiatric admissions to the hospital. High-volume users of these services are people with severe and persistent mental illness (SPMI), which is a diagnosis of nonorganic psychosis of personality disorder. An SPMI is characterized as prolonged illness, which often requires long-term treatment and often results in disability (Rosedale & Bigio, 2008).

The Brokerage Model

One model of behavioral health case management is the Brokerage Model, which involves a case manager who coordinates care among all involved parties. This model has an extended form, where leadership is assumed by mental health professionals who are actively involved in the patient's care. A psychiatrist is often the leader of the interdisciplinary team. This model is designed to provide services for individuals with SPMIs. The functions of the case manager include:

A. Patient advocacy
B. Transportation of consumers to and from treatment sites
C. Symptom and medication monitoring
D. Assessment and teaching regarding community living
E. Initiation and coordination of referrals, benefits, and entitlements (Rosedale & Bigio, 2008)

The Strengths Model

The Strengths Model differs from the Brokerage Model in that most services are provided outside an office setting. Staff services include broad areas of:

- Engagement – This includes identification of achievements, aspirations and interests of the patient, sensitivity to patient's preferences, and use of the case manager's self-disclosure.
- Personal planning – This focuses on the measurable steps made toward achieving what the patient desires.
- Strengths assessment – This involves prioritizing the patient's past and present accomplishments, resources, and future interests.
- Resource acquisition – This requires designing activities with the patient to increase contact with community resources (Rosedale & Bigio, 2008).

The Assertive Community Treatment (ACT) Model

The Assertive Community Treatment (ACT) Model is the most recognized and articulate model used by case managers and healthcare facilities. Research shows that this model controls psychiatric symptoms, reduces hospital use, increases housing stability, and improves quality of life. The key elements of the ACT Model include:

- Shared caseloads
- Team-delivered services
- Caseload of 10 patients
- Services provided in the community setting
- Seven-day operation
- Capability of responding to patient crises
- Controlled rate of admissions
- Competent interdisciplinary team

- Team support and debriefing (Rosedale & Bigio, 2008)

Psychosocial, Neuropsychological, and Cultural Assessment

The Psychosocial Assessment

The psychosocial assessment is a critical part of the case management process. The case manager must treat the whole family unit regarding the patient's needs and preferences. Questions to consider when assessing psychosocial aspects include:

- What stresses are occurring that affect the patient's life and the family unit during the illness? This includes divorce, death in the family, job change or loss, moving, or a new baby.
- How does the family cope with stress? Some methods include meditation, religious activities, sports, exercise, talking with friends or a counselor, physical violence, anger, or use of substances.
- Who lives in the home? Some patients are responsible for the care of an elderly parent or ill spouse.
- Does the family unit require respite care? This involves an assessment for exhaustion and/or burn-out.
- Does the patient have hobbies or participate in recreational activities? The case manager needs to assess to see if the patient has lost his/her primary form of entertainment.
- Is there adequate formal support? This involves assessing for dysfunctional or inadequate support systems.
- Is there a need for job or school placement? This involves assessing for necessary school and job-related issues.
- Can the patient return to the previous living situation or environment? This includes the need for short- or long-term skilled nursing care or placement in a rehabilitation center.
- Are there secondary gains to the patient's illness? Because of conscious or unconscious needs, some patients do not desire to get well. Many individuals like the special attention they receive from healthcare providers and family (Powell & Tahan, 2010).

The Neuropsychological Assessment

Depression among elderly patients occurs with many conditions that decrease quality of life such as arthritis, cancer, neuromuscular diseases, stroke, heart disease, diabetes, and Huntington's disease. Many drugs can precipitate depression such as cimetidine, hydralazine, corticosteroids, drugs for Parkinson's disease, diuretics, propranolol, and digitalis. Symptoms of depression include changes in appetite, increased fatigue, sadness, loss of interest in usual activities, anxiety, and sleep disturbances (Rittenmeyer, 2010).

The Cultural Assessment

The first step in a cultural assessment is to establish trust by respecting the patient's cultural values and traditions, making careful observations, and listening to the patient's concerns. Cultural assessment is part of a psychosocial evaluation, so asking permission and explaining the purpose of it is not necessary. For some ethnic groups, taking notes while talking is considered rude, so the case manager should explain the purpose of the notes and should maintain focus on the patient and family instead of paperwork (Rittenmeyer, 2010).

Special Considerations

For some patients, the hospital is a safe place where another person cannot abuse them. When the case manager encounters this problem, it is necessary to offer a psychiatric consultation and possible referrals to outpatient resources and support groups. If the patient is homeless, the case manager must attempt to find temporary housing in a homeless shelter or other facility (Powell & Tahan, 2010).

The Brick Wall Syndrome

The brick wall syndrome is a psychosocial situation where a patient requires intensive care, and family members insist they can provide this at home. When the family members "hit the brick wall," they realize they are unable to care for the patient in the home setting and request a long-term care facility. When the case manager suspects that home placement will not succeed, he/she should make necessary preparations for patient placement in a hospital setting, just in case it is needed (Powell & Tahan, 2010).

Poverty

Poverty is a risk factor for malnutrition because many individuals cannot afford to purchase nutritious foods. Other risk factors for malnutrition include a recent weight gain or loss of ten pounds or more, ill-fitting dentures, lack of teeth, dental caries, tooth abscesses, living alone, and a history of eating disorders.

Poverty presents many challenges to the provision of optimal palliative care for the terminally ill and dying patient. Many patients who live in poverty have unstable or nonexistent housing, making "home" care quite difficult. The lack of dependable transportation can encumber scheduled medical visits and urgent care services. Also, patients who live in poverty often do not have basic needs such as shelter, food, and a stable support system. However, patients living in poverty do not always have less effective coping skills. As with other socioeconomic groups, these patients have a wide range of psychological reactions to the dying process and end-of-life issues. Many patients who struggle to meet basic human needs are flexible, resilient, and pragmatic when faced with challenges.

Situational Crises

For many patients, a serious illness and hospitalization constitutes a crisis. A crisis is the overwhelming events or series of events that create a situation that is perceived as threatening or unbearable. A situational crisis occurs when the unexpected event causes stress to a person or family such as the development of an acute illness. The developmental stages of a crisis include:

- The person or family is in a state of homeostasis.
- The stressful event occurs.
- Well-known coping skills fail to reduce the threat.
- A period of disequilibrium occurs.
- The problem is either resolved, or personal disintegration occurs (Rittenmeyer, 2010).

A situational crisis is where the problem leads to the disruption of normal psychological functioning. Examples of a situational crisis include an unwanted pregnancy, a new baby, divorce, death of a loved one, onset of or change in a disease process, loss of job or career, and being a victim of a violent act. Community situational crises are events that affect an entire community. These include terrorist attacks, floods, hurricanes, earthquakes, and tornadoes (Rittenmeyer, 2010).

Palliative Care

Palliative care begins when the patient is diagnosed with a life-threatening disease or terminal illness such as advanced cancer or end-stage renal disease. Many patients are referred to palliative care when they have serious chronic diseases even though death does not appear imminent. The patient's request alone for this service is not adequate without the proper diagnosis. Also, palliative care is often supportive in the early stages, but will intensify as the patient's condition worsens (Wraa, Coulter, & Kelly, 2010).

Monitoring Tests and Tools

- The Pain Assessment in Advanced Dementia (PAINAD) Scale – This tool utilizes careful observation of non-verbal behavior to evaluate pain. Changes are noted in:
  - Vocalization – Includes moaning, negative speech, absent speech, and crying
  - Respirations – Involves rapid and labored breathing with short periods of Cheyne-Stokes respiration or hyperventilation
  - Body language – Involves tension, fidgeting, clenching fists, pacing, and lying in a fetal position
  - Consolability – Where the patient is less easily distractible or not consolable

- The Confusion Assessment Method – This tool is used to assess the development of delirium and is used by healthcare workers without psychiatric training. The nine factors of this tool are:
  - Onset – Acute changes in mental status
  - Attention – Inattentive, stable, or fluctuating
  - Thinking – Rambling, switching topics, illogical, and/or rambling
  - Orientation – To time, person, and place
  - Level of consciousness – Altered or within normal limits
  - Memory – Impaired or intact
  - Perceptional disturbances – Illusions and hallucinations
  - Psychomotor abnormalities – Agitation or retardation
  - Sleep-wake cycle – Awake at night and asleep during the day

- The Mini-Cog Test – This tool assesses for dementia with two components:
  - Drawing the face of a clock with all 12 numbers and both hands to show the time specified
  - Repeating the names of three common objects that are given early in the interview process

- The Mini-Mental Status Exam – This tool assesses cognition through:
  - Naming items
  - Counting backward from 100 by sevens or spelling a word backwards
  - Remembering and later repeating the names of three well-known objects
  - Copying a picture of interlocking shapes
  - Following simple, three-part instructions (Rittenmeyer, 2010)

Psychosocial Aspects of Chronic Illness and Disability

Chronic illness can be present at any age. The psychological, physical, and social realities of sustained illness often result in typical consequences with chronic illnesses. These illnesses are insidious, irreversible, and require much time and energy of family members, healthcare providers, and the chronically ill patient. Most chronic illnesses follow courses that change over time, and the trajectory of that course is what the community-based case manager attempts to alter, improve, or change (Scott & Boyd, 2005).

Evaluation of the chronically ill patient requires analyzing the trajectories to consider how and when the healthcare system is accessed. Chronic illness involves a complex set of relationships and various systems to support them such as the community-based nurse case management model. This model uses nurse case managers as key enablers of care for those who are chronically ill. It has shown success related to cost-effective healthcare utilization. Community-based case management has expanded in the last decade, and this method is used for a variety of patient populations. Most of these programs address patient needs and increase quality of care (Scott & Boyd, 2005).

Jung's theory is called the Theory of Individualism. This theory holds that one's personality continues to develop during the course of a lifespan. Personality comprises personal unconsciousness, collective unconsciousness, and ego. Also, personality is both introverted and extroverted, with a balance needed for adequate emotional health. Jung proposed that, during middle age, people begin to question their beliefs, values, and attainments, and they turn inward as they continue to age. Successful aging involves the value of one's self outweighing the concern for external things, physical limitations, and losses (Rittenmeyer, 2010).

Management of Patients with Substance Use, Abuse, and Addiction

Substance and alcohol use, abuse, and addiction are all part of a maladaptive pattern of alcohol and narcotics use. Abuse is manifested by recurrent and significant adverse consequences within a 12-month time period. Substance dependence occurs by repeated self-administration of substances that cause tolerance, withdrawal, and compulsive drug-taking behavior. People with alcohol abuse also show a maladaptive pattern of alcohol consumption that results in adverse consequences during a 12-month time period. For both narcotics and alcohol abuse, these consequences include:

- Recurrent substance use in situations where it can be hazardous such as driving
- Failure to fulfill role obligations at school, work, or home such as repeated absences
- Recurrent use-related legal problems such as disorderly conduct arrest
- Continued use of substance despite substance-caused social and interpersonal problems such as divorce or altercations (Rosedale & Bigio, 2008)

The treatment of patients with substance-related diagnoses involves assessment and diagnosis of those patients with dual diagnoses. Also, patients who are under the influence of mind-altering substances cannot be accurately diagnosed until the effects have been eliminated. Once the patient is diagnosed, he/she must receive treatment for both conditions (Rosedale & Bigio, 2008).

Dual diagnosis is the term that refers to combined substance abuse and a mental health disorder. The initial treatment for a dual diagnosis involves detoxification from drugs so the mental health condition can be accurately assessed. After detoxification, the patient undergoes rehabilitation and mental health treatment, which involves the use of medications and/or therapy (Trigoboff, 2010).

Patients who experience an unintentional overdose should be referred for a psychosocial evaluation because the overdose could have occurred from an inability to read instructions, polypharmacy, excessive use of medications, and/or lack of knowledge. Other indications for a psychosocial evaluation include chronic mental illness, eating disorders, substance abuse, intentional overdose, and dementia. Heart diseases, homelessness, and limited financial resources do not readily indicate the need for a psychosocial evaluation (Trigoboff, 2010).

The CAGE assessment tool assesses for abuse of alcohol. The "C" indicates "cutting down," the "A" indicates "annoyed at criticism," the "G" indicates "guilty feelings," and the "E" indicates "eye opener." Answering "yes" to one question on the CAGE questionnaire suggests the possibility of a drinking problem, and answering "yes" to two or more of these questions indicates an actual drinking problem (Trigoboff, 2010).

Spirituality and End-of-Life Issues

Spirituality and religion often play a key role with how the injured or ill patient experiences or responds to the condition or the dying process. One important part of the patient assessment is to evaluate the role of religious beliefs. Some patients are active in a religious community, whereas others may have their own personal beliefs and not attend an official community church or organization. Spiritual beliefs can affect the patient's willingness to pursue treatment and service as potential sources of comfort during the dying process (Wraa, Coulter, & Kelly, 2010).

Religion and spirituality may play a major role in a patient's terminally ill experience, and these concepts affect how that person responds to the dying process. Assessing the role of spiritual or religious beliefs is an important component of the psychosocial assessment and should take place as early as possible in the palliative care case manager-patient relationship. Patients who do not identify strongly with religious or spiritual beliefs should not be urged to do so (Wraa, Coulter, & Kelly, 2010).

End-of-life care is provided by the healthcare team during the last few weeks and months of a person's life. This is necessary when he/she is experiencing an end-stage illness that is steadily progressing toward the death stage. End-of-life care is an integrated patient and family-centered approach to healthcare, which is guided by a sense of respect for the patient's comfort and dignity (Wraa, Coulter, & Kelly, 2010).

Bereavement, Mourning, and Grief

Bereavement is the time period of mourning. The amount of time varies from person to person, but is typically 6-12 months or longer. Grief is a normal response to loss, and mourning is the public expression of grief. The three types of grief are acute, chronic, and anticipatory. With chronic grief, the person is at risk for depression, which is characterized by feelings of sadness and changes in mood (Wraa, Coulter, & Kelly, 2010).

The Durable Power of Attorney

During the dying process, the terminally ill patient often lacks the mental capacity to make end-of-life treatment decisions. Family members often become the primary medical decision-makers in the absence of a durable power of attorney. Many conflicts arise concerning the dying process due to varying values and opinions among the family members. Members of the palliative care team should encourage family members to do what they believe the patient would have wanted if he/she was able to make these decisions (Wraa, Coulter, & Kelly, 2010).

The durable power of attorney is a legal document that designates a person to make decisions regarding all medical and end-of-life care when a patient is mentally incompetent. This document is a type of advanced directive, which also includes specific requests from the patient regarding treatment and living wills. A Do Not Resuscitate (DNR) order is a document that indicates the patient does not want to be resuscitated for a terminal condition or illness. A general power of attorney allows one designated person to make broad decisions for the patient (Wraa, Coulter, & Kelly, 2010).

A patient or parent's refusal of care can be overridden in a few specific instances. These include when the patient is mentally incompetent to make decisions even though advanced directives were established prior to the onset of dementia and when refusing care puts the general public at risk such as with treatment for highly communicable diseases (Wraa, Coulter, & Kelly, 2010).

Intravenous hydration is considered a medical intervention in the U.S., so it can be refused if the patient or family feels it is a burden. The administration of intravenous hydration to a dying patient should be determined based on the patient's goals and symptoms. Family members and caregivers often find it emotionally difficult to not provide hydration to a dying person. Dehydration can often lead to improvement with certain symptoms associated with the dying process such as edema, vomiting, and respiratory congestion (Wraa, Coulter, & Kelly, 2010).

Support Groups and Community Resources

A key component to case management is the ability to locate and utilize support groups and community resources. These services increase patient adherence to medical regimens. Patient education should involve etiology and progression of the disease, precipitation of signs and symptoms of impending problems, medication information, dietary considerations, and lifestyle modifications (Alvarado & Sunderland, 2008).

Resources for Elder Care

- American Association of Retired Persons (AARP) – This organization has information on every aspect of aging and is a resource for case managers and patients.
- Area Agency on Aging (AAA) – This agency offers a variety of programs including referral to hands-on support programs.
- Local public health departments – These departments can provide in-home visits by public health nurses for activities associated with health promotion.

- American Society on Aging – This organization has a large library of educational materials for case managers and patients. It also sponsors conferences for case managers and other healthcare providers to attend.
- Services organizations – These include the Salvation Army and the St. Vincent DePaul Society. These organizations offer programs for the elderly such as friendly visitor programs, adult day health programs, free or low-cost transportation, and equipment loan programs (Alvarado & Sunderland, 2008).

Resources for Maternal-Infant Care

The maternal-infant case management program is linked intricately to the community. The maternal-infant case manager must be able to identify community resources within the neighborhood of the mother and infant; determine access to and availability of these services; evaluate community transportation for access to the necessary healthcare; and incorporate strategies into the community through volunteer outreach, educational programs, and community coalitions (Davis, 2008).

To increase the mother's support system, the case manager must coordinate patient education efforts. Prenatal classes are offered by many healthcare facilities and nonprofit organizations. Also, Lamaze classes should be encouraged. Many HMOs offer educational programs for new mothers and prenatal screening for pregnant women. These programs offer information materials such as booklets, tapes, brochures, and books. Many HMO programs offer incentives to their plan participants for early prenatal care, bimonthly visits, and/or participation in a perinatal wellness program (Davis, 2008).

In this situation, it is most appropriate to refer a single mother to a social worker with the expertise to provide assistance of this nature. Social workers can assist patients with such programs as Temporary Assistance for Needy Families (TANF) and food stamps. Also, the social worker can help the patient avoid homelessness by assisting with subsidized and low-cost housing.

Resources for Children

There are numerous resources and support systems available to help children and their families such as churches, employers, civic groups, friends, and relatives. Also, there are many local and national chapters of organizations that offer help to children. These include:

- The March of Dimes
- The American Cancer Society
- Cystic Fibrosis Foundation
- The National Head Injury Foundation
- Easter Seals
- Make-a-Wish Foundation
- SIDS Foundation

- The Spina Bifida Association
- Association for Retarded Citizens
- United Cerebral Palsy Association
- The American Lung Association (Davis, 2008)

There are many state-sponsored Title V programs that help patients and families obtain specialized rehabilitation and medical services, assistive technology, DME, and medical supplies. These programs vary from state to state, and eligibility is typically based on financial need (Davis, 2008).

Family Dynamics

Several indicators need to be evaluated and addressed concerning the family of the technology-dependent or medically fragile child. Family members often experience adverse consequences when a child has a chronic condition. Indicators of child health outcomes include income, employment, parental health, sibling health, sibling adaption, family interaction, and family support. The family unit depends on the level of family support provided through the case management care plan such as psychological and social support, respite care, and crisis intervention (Davis, 2008).

When a child is sick, each member of the family is affected to some degree. Many family units are blended, whereas others are extended. The case manager must establish the primary caregiver, which is usually the child's mother or father. The primary caregiver is the one who is responsible for learning all aspects of the child's care. The case manager needs to assess the caregiver's readiness and willingness to learn, motivation level, and ability to learn (Davis, 2008).

Chapter 4: Healthcare Management and Delivery

This section covers clinical settings for case management, disease management, the Medical Home Model, palliative care and symptom management, rehabilitation service delivery systems, transitional planning, continuum of care, critical pathways, standards of care and practice guidelines, the Chronic Care Model, and the interdisciplinary care team.

Clinical Settings for Case Management

Medical Unit

Medical units most often require the services of a case manager. Medical patients usually are older people who have complex discharge plans. These patients are not easily able to advocate for themselves, so they are often overlooked during and after an extended hospital stay. Each medical unit case manager typically has an average caseload of 20-25 patients. Criteria for patient selection on a general medical unit are determined through a retrospective audit of those patients who have patterns of increased resource usage. Also, patients who would benefit from case management services include those:

- Over 70 years old
- With potential for falls
- With a potential for skin breakdown
- With noncompliance with treatment
- With home care needs
- With a complicated medical plan
- With complicated teaching needs
- With discharge placement issues (Cohen & Cesta, 2005)

Surgical Unit

Surgical unit patients are often complicated, but their hospital course is more predictable and amendable to a predetermined plan than medical patients. Most surgeons have protocols to manage the surgical patient's postoperative hospital stay and home care. The surgical case manager often carries a larger caseload than does a medical case manager, with a range of 25-30 patients. Accelerated turnover of patients means that the workload for the surgical case manager is equivalent to that of the medical case manager. Criteria for patient selection on the surgical unit are based on patient need, case complexity, and severity of illness or condition (Cohen & Cesta, 2005).

Critical Care Unit

The critical care unit has a low nurse to patient ratio, so these patients often receive a different form of case management. In critical care, case managers can help with clinical management issues such as admission and discharge. Most critical care case management plans are created with particular clinical problems in mind such as ventilator weaning. Also, cardiology and surgical intensive care case managers are often responsible for the critical care unit. Emergency department case managers can assist with critical care unit patients by expediting treatment and admissions of those admitted to the unit from the emergency department (Cohen & Cesta, 2005).

Skilled Nursing Facility

The skilled nursing facility is a non-acute care organization that benefits from a case management system. A case manager can ensure a higher quality of patient care and improvement in safety protocols and patient outcomes. Skilled nursing facilities are required to provide plans of care with set goals for the residents. Regulation specifies that an RN be present for most instances, but this professional can also be an educator, coordinator of services, or facilitator of case management (Cohen & Cesta, 2005).

Sub-acute Care Facility

Sub-acute care is a level of care that blends long-term care with acute care skills and philosophies. Sub-acute care facilities often bridge acute and long-term care, and the patient stay is shorter than in a skilled nursing facility. Most patients are admitted to these facilities following a hospitalization, and models include short-term medically complex, short-term rehabilitative, and chronic. Short-term medically complex patients are typically postsurgical patients or those with complex medical conditions, but who are stable. Short-term rehabilitative patients are those with potential for improvement, but still have significant nursing needs and are unable to tolerate intense rehabilitation. Chronic care patients have an extended acute care stay, are medically stable, and require high ancillary and/or nursing care (Cohen & Cesta, 2005).

Ambulatory and Outpatient Facilities

Case managers are often used in ambulatory and outpatient facilities. This is related to the implementation of prospective payment for emergency departments, hospital-based clinics, urgent care centers, and ambulatory surgery centers. Patients receive coordinated and cost-effective care with the help of a case manager, and case management services assist with communication and continuity of care. The case management plan in an ambulatory or outpatient facility is developed based on each patient's expected outcomes. This approach is often used for clinic visits, home care visits, outpatient surgery visits, and urgent care visits (Cohen & Cesta, 2005).

Disease Management

Disease management (DM) is a system of coordinated healthcare interventions and communications for patients of a certain population and with conditions in which patient self-care efforts are similar. A disease management model is a holistic care model that concerns patients of a particular population. Disease state case management (DSCM) is a population-based approach to healthcare that identifies patients with chronic diseases, evaluates their health status, initiates a plan of care, and gathers data to evaluate the effectiveness of this process (Powell & Tahan, 2008).

Purpose of a Disease Management Program

Disease management programs are implemented for a variety of reasons such as:

- To prevent fragmentation of care – The component management model of healthcare involves numerous providers who are the "components" along the continuum. Disease management can support education and preventive care to reduce hospitalizations and emergency care visits.
- To eliminate financial pressures – Disease-specific healthcare spending is one cost pressure that case management eliminates. Also, this service assists with the risk-sharing process.
- To prevent exacerbation of disease – Disease management is a comprehensive, integrated approach to reimbursement and care based on a disease's natural course.
- To designate prospectively determined interventions – This is done to alter the disease course, improve clinical and financial outcomes, and enhance quality of life (Powell & Tahan, 2008).

Components of a Disease Management Program

- Comprehension of the disease course and application of evidence-based guidelines – The case manager must evaluate relevant data to determine core issues, such as causes, patterns of symptoms, and quality drivers. Also, disease management involves prevention of exacerbation and complications from the disease.
- Identification of patients who would benefit from a DM program – Finding high-risk patients before they become ill is dependent on predictive modeling. The primary goal with this approach is to initiate proactive case management. Three statistical techniques used with predictive modeling include rules-based techniques, regression techniques, and neural network technology.
- Focus on diagnosis and treatment of the disease – This involves the appropriate allocation of resources and the use of those that support evidence-based disease treatment options.
- Focus on prevention of exacerbation – This involves educational efforts, use of preventive complementary and alternative medicine (CAM) modalities, and health promotion activities.

- Increase in patient adherence to medical regimens – This involves patient education of etiology, disease progression, precipitating reasons, signs and symptoms, dietary considerations, lifestyle modifications, and follow-up appointments.
- Use of telehealth – This involves the use of telemonitoring to deliver health-related services and information via electronic and web-based technologies.
- Establishment of integrated data management systems for outcome measurement and process assessment – This involves measuring outcomes through sophisticated software systems. Outcomes from the DM program could include reduced hospitalizations and emergency department visits, decreased healthcare expenses, increased patient satisfaction, improved access to healthcare services, and improved disease-specific clinical outcomes (Powell & Tahan, 2008).

The Disease Management/Case Management Process

1. Identify at-risk patients – Use criteria to assess high-risk patients for select diseases. Potential sources of information include pharmacy data, encounter data, hospital utilization patterns, and claims and billing data.
2. Assess and evaluate patients – This involves psychosocial issues, financial factors, competency barriers to self-care, disease-specific clinical details, and severity of target disease state (priority 1, 2, or 3).
3. Develop DM plans – Use evidence-based practice guidelines to establish goals and objectives.
4. Implement DM plans – This involves ongoing monitoring and assessment of the patient's condition, referrals to specialists as necessary, and involvement of the patient and family in the DM program.
5. Evaluate outcome measures – Use clinical and quality indicators to assess outcomes and use cost indicators to assess financial outcomes (Powell & Tahan, 2008).

Medical Home Model

A "medical home" refers to a healthcare model in which individuals use primary care practices to provide comprehensive, accessible, and continuous care. The goal of the Medical Home Model is to give a patient several options of care including preventive and curative. With this model, care is provided over a period of time. There are currently three trends building momentum for the Medical Home Model: the aging population, the increased prevalence of chronic diseases, and the growing shortage of primary care providers. This model has the potential to lower overall U.S. healthcare costs, but the system currently lacks incentives concerning chronic care coordination and preventive health programs (Deloitte Center for Health Solutions, 2013).

The Patient-Centered Primary Care Collaborative (PCPCC)

The Patient-Centered Primary Care Collaborative (PCPCC) describes the medical home as an alternative approach to primary care delivery that is:

- Comprehensive – A team of healthcare providers is accountable for the patient's physical and mental healthcare needs.
- Patient-centered – There is a partnership among patients, families, and providers to ensure that decisions meet the patient's wants, needs, and preferences and that the patient receives the support and teaching needed to make these decisions.
- Coordinated – Care is organized across all elements of the healthcare system including specialty care, primary care, hospital care, home healthcare, community services, and necessary support services.
- Accessible – Patients can access services with shorter wait times, through 24/7 telephonic or electronic means, with after-hours services, and by use of good communication through health informatics technology.
- Committed – Providers and healthcare staff are committed to quality and safety through the use of health informatics technology and other tools that allow patients and families to make informed decisions regarding their health and healthcare (Patient-Centered Primary Care Collaborative, 2013).

Elements of PCMH Recognition

The National Committee for Quality Assurance (NCQA) Physician Practice Connections and Patient-Centered Medical Home (PPC-PCMH) Recognition Program developed the Medical Home Model in 2003 with the support from many professional organizations. For an organization or facility to achieve PCMH Recognition, specific elements must be met. These are:

- ELEMENT 1A: Access and communication processes – The practice has written processes for scheduling appointments and communicating with patients.
- ELEMENT 1B: Access and communication results – The practice has data showing that it meets the standards in element 1A for scheduling and communicating with patients.
- ELEMENT 2D: Organizing clinical data – The practice uses electronic or paper-based charting tools to organize and document clinical information.
- ELEMENT 2E: Identifying important conditions – The practice uses an electronic or paper-based system to identify the following in the practice's patient population:
  - Most frequently seen diagnoses
  - Most important risk factors
  - Three clinically important conditions

- ELEMENT 3A: Guidelines for important conditions – The practice must implement evidence-based guidelines for the three identified clinically important conditions.
- ELEMENT 4B: Self-management support – The practice works to facilitate self-management of care for patients with one of the three clinically important conditions.
- ELEMENT 6A: Test tracking and follow-up – The practice works to improve effectiveness of care by managing the timely receipt of information on all tests and results.
- ELEMENT 7A: Referral tracking – The practice seeks to improve effectiveness, timeliness, and coordination of care by following through on critical consultations with other practitioners.
- ELEMENT 8A: Measures of performance – The practice measures or receives performance data by physician or across the practice regarding:
  - Clinical process
  - Clinical outcomes
  - Service data
  - Patient safety
- ELEMENT 8C: Reporting to physicians – The practice reports on its performance on the factors in element 8A (National Committee on Quality Assurance, 2013).

Palliative Care and Symptom Management

Palliative care begins when a patient is diagnosed with a life-threatening or terminal disease, such as amyotrophic lateral sclerosis (ALS), advanced cancer, or end-stage renal disease (ESRD). Even though death is not immediately imminent, patients with other serious chronic diseases, such as chronic obstructive pulmonary disease (COPD) or cirrhosis of the liver, can be referred for palliative care. A patient's request for palliative care may not support the diagnosis, however. The impact of increased healthcare costs and decreased insurance coverage has made the need for palliative and hospice services stronger. Also, the number of palliative care programs has grown in the last couple of decades (Correoso & Santiago, 2008).

Palliative care is a philosophy of care and a highly structured care delivery system. It is a process where an interdisciplinary team attempts to end suffering and enhance quality of life for people with advanced diseases and end-stage illnesses. The delivery of palliative care services requires the knowledge and skills of healthcare providers who have training in care of the terminally ill (Correoso & Santiago, 2008).

Principles and Goals of a Palliative Care Program

- Provision of information to support decisions related to care
- Showing respect to the patient and family regarding values, preferences, and cultural and social beliefs

- Care and services given by an interdisciplinary team and coordinated by a case manager
- Total needs of the patient and family addressed, such as symptom control; psychological distress; legal, social, practical, and financial ramifications; and spiritual issues
- Care and services administered across various settings of a continuum of care
- Healthcare providers and palliative professionals advocating for the patient and family (Correoso & Santiago, 2008)

Examples of End-Stage Disease Indicators

Core Indicators	Physical decline Weight loss Multiple comorbidities
Heart Disease	Ejection fraction < 20% Arrhythmias resistant to treatment Discomfort with physical activity
Liver Disease	PT > 5 sec Ascites resistant to treatment Hepatorenal syndrome
Renal Disease	Intractable fluid overload Oliguria < 40 cc/24 hr Hyperkalemia
Pulmonary Disease	Dyspnea at rest Recurrent lung infections pO2 < 55 mmG and O2 sat < 88%
Cerebrovascular Accident	Paralysis post-stroke dementia Medical complications persistent Nutritional decline

Amyotrophic Lateral Sclerosis	Unable to walk
	Difficulty swallowing
	Dyspnea at rest on O2 (Correoso & Santiago, 2008)

Rehabilitation Service Delivery Systems

Rehabilitation is the restoration of handicapped persons to their fullest physical, mental, vocational, social, and economic usefulness through the implementation and coordination of comprehensive services deemed necessary. Rehabilitation services are provided in acute care hospitals, rehabilitation centers, sub-acute care facilities, long-term care facilities, comprehensive outpatient rehabilitation facilities (CORFs), day rehabilitation services (DRSs), and home rehabilitation through home health agencies (Schoenbeck, Tahan, & Powell, 2008).

Rehabilitation Healthcare Providers

There are many healthcare providers who participate with the interdisciplinary team to provide rehabilitation services. The team sets both short- and long-term treatment goals for the patient. The team members include:

- Physicians – Includes a physiatrist who specializes in rehabilitation and physical medicine
- Internist/specialist physicians – Depends on the patient's condition
- Nurses – Those who practice rehabilitation nursing
- Physical therapists
- Occupational therapists
- Speech and language pathologists
- Dietitians
- Social workers
- Psychologists and psychiatrists
- Case managers (Schoenbeck, Tahan, & Powell, 2008)

Insurance Requirements for Rehabilitation

For the insurance company to cover rehabilitation services and treatment, there are two fundamental requirements that must be met:

- The care must be reasonable and necessary as related to duration, frequency, efficacy, and amount.
- The care must be reasonable and necessary to provide the care in an inpatient setting rather than in a less-intensive facility (Schoenbeck, Tahan, & Powell, 2008).

Rehabilitation care may occur in healthcare facilities and centers that are dedicated to the provision of these services, are staffed by rehabilitation professionals, have 24-hour physician coverage, and include an interdisciplinary team that meets weekly or more frequently to evaluate and discuss the patient's process and plan of care. Also, the team must develop an individualized program of rehabilitation for the patient that involves at least three hours of therapy each day. The goal of this therapy is to reduce or reverse an impairment, handicap, or disability so the patient can achieve the fullest functional capacity possible (Schoenbeck, Tahan, & Powell, 2008).

Milliman Care Guidelines

The Milliman Care Guidelines are now called the General Recovery Care Guidelines. They cover a wide range of topics for various levels of patient care. General recovery guidelines are used with patients who have complex medical situations that do not fit into other guidelines. These guidelines are based on specific information used by case managers to determine appropriate care, including:

- Evidence-based treatment for complex cases – Uses the best evidence related to comorbidities, complications, and complex diagnoses and symptoms
- Long-term acute care hospital (LTACH) care – Contains clinical indications for admission to a LTACH
- Problem-oriented general recovery – Includes detailed clinical indications for admission when a patient has multiple conditions, illnesses or traumas, or other systemic problems
- Case management – Used for ambulatory surgery, behavioral healthcare, medical care, and surgical care
- Home and recovery facility care – Guidance on clinical indications for admission to home care and rehabilitation facilities (Milliman Care Guidelines, 2013)

Transitional Planning

Transitional planning is based on the "continuity of care" concept. Case management is involved with transitional planning in that the case manager helps transition patients from one level of care to another. The transition involves maintaining quality of care and access to services. CMS developed the Conditions of Participation (CoP), which are standards that healthcare facilities must meet to participate in government insurance programs. These standards improve quality and protect the safety and well-being of health plan members. The CoP standards apply to patients receiving services regarding discharge planning, medical records, and patient rights (Birmingham, 2008).

Case Manager's Role in Transitional Planning

The provider-based case manager is responsible for transitional planning and discharge of patients from organizations that provide or manage the care of patients who receive medical or nursing services. These include hospitals, nursing facilities, psychiatric facilities, inpatient rehabilitation facilities, home healthcare agencies, and hospice organizations. Functions of the case manager include:

- Identification of individuals who are at risk for potential adverse outcomes during the transition or discharge from one level of care to another
- Evaluation of continuing care needs of the patient
- Assessment of appropriate and available resources
- Implementation of the transition plan
- Monitoring and reassessment of the transition plan
- Documentation of pertinent information related to the transitional plan or discharge
- Identification of admission criteria for necessary level of care
- Advocacy for patient rights, values, and needs to ensure values, beliefs, and preferences are respected and considered during the discharge/transition period
- Collaboration with the interdisciplinary team
- Coordination of care and discharge plans
- Validation that ordered care and services for the next level of care are reasonably assured
- Education of patient and family concerning the transition phase of care
- Protection of privacy of healthcare information
- Report of abuse, abandonment, neglect, or exploitation of the patient
- Evaluation of the patient's decision-making capabilities
- Assurance of quality improvement and assurance initiatives and activities (Birmingham, 2008)

Handoffs and Handovers

Also called handover, handoff of a patient from one level is part of transition of care. This may occur within the healthcare facility when a patient transfers from one unit to another or between two facilities. Transition of care also involves a change in the plan of care or health plan. A handoff may involve a formal checklist for acceptance or a formal sign-off sheet (Birmingham, 2008).

Reintegration into the Community

For reintegration into the community, a patient who has suffered a serious injury or illness requires a comprehensive plan of care. Issues addressed in this plan include financial support, job training, housing, family support, medical assistance, assistive technology, environmental modifications, follow-up and continued services, and safety. The goals for reintegration must be realistic and have time frames based on patient activities and skills. The case manager must be aware of all necessary services, available resources, and needed referrals (Birmingham, 2008).

Discharge Planning

Discharge planning is a process of assessing a patient's needs after discharge from a healthcare facility and putting the necessary services in place before discharge. The case manager will ensure a safe discharge to the next level of care or setting, provide appropriate resources for ongoing care, and ensure a timely and safe transition. The disposition of the patient at discharge is called the discharge status, and it indicates what level of care the patient is going to receive. The discharge status indicates how the healthcare facility will be paid using specific codes assigned to various dispositions (Birmingham, 2008).

Discharge Disposition Codes

Code	Description
01	Discharged to home (routine discharge): Includes discharge to home on oxygen or DME services without home health, law enforcement, residential care, or foster care
02	Discharged to short-term healthcare facility for inpatient care: Code used to bill a same-day transfer claim for an inpatient claim
03	Discharged to skilled nursing facility (SNF) with Medicare certification: Indicates the patient qualifies for skilled care
04	Discharged to intermediate care facility (ICF): Indicates the patient requires nursing care in state-designated assisted living facility
05	Discharged to institution not otherwise specified: Includes cancer and children's hospitals
06	Discharged to home under care of home health service organization for skilled care: Patient goes home with a written home care plan of services
07	Left against medical advice or discontinued care: These claims treated as transfers when the patient is subsequently admitted to another inpatient facility
20	Expired
43	Discharged to federal hospital: Used when the patient goes to the VA hospital or other federal facility
50	Discharged to hospice (home)
51	Discharged to hospice (medical facility)
61	Discharged to hospital-based Medicare-approved swing bed
62	Discharged to rehabilitation facility
63	Discharged to long-term care facility
64	Discharged to nursing facility certified under Medicaid, but not Medicare
65	Discharged to psychiatric hospital or unit
66	Discharged to critical access hospital (Centers for Medicare & Medicaid Services, 2005)

Continuum of Care

Continuum of care is a concept that involves an integrated system of care to guide and track a patient over time through a comprehensive method that covers all levels of care. Most traditional healthcare promotion initiatives focus on primary and secondary models. Common intervention tools include preventive screenings, risk assessment, risk reduction, and self-care education. Many measures focus on chronological patterns of care, but do not directly measure continuity or any of the aspects of care associated with connection and coherence (Haggerty, Reid, Freeman, Starfield, & Adair, 2003).

Facilities for Continuum of Care

To facilitate the continuum of care after a patient is discharged from an acute care facility, the case manager should establish relationships with staff of skilled nursing facilities, home health agencies, sub-acute care facilities, rehabilitation centers, group homes, and assisted living facilities. In group homes and assisted living facilities, the patients can usually manage self-care with minimal supervision. These licensed facilities usually house four to eight patients with similar conditions and illnesses (Birmingham, 2008).

Types of Continuity

Continuity of care in case management is best achieved when discrete elements in the care pathway are connected regardless of different episodes, interventions by many providers, or changes in the patient's health status. According to Haggerty and colleagues (2003), there are three types of continuity in every discipline:

- Information Continuity – Because information is a common thread that links care from one healthcare provider to another and from one health-related event to another, it is accumulated so that people can interact to provide necessary healthcare to patients. Knowledge about the patient is accumulated in the providers' memories and the medical record.
- Management Continuity – For chronic and complex clinical diseases, management continuity is especially relevant. This form of continuity is achieved when services are conducted in a timely and complementary manner. Management continuity is facilitated by shared care protocols that provide a sense of security and predictability. One important aspect of this type of continuity is flexibility in adapting care to changes in the patient's circumstances and/or needs.
- Relational Continuity – This type of continuity bridges past care to current care, providing a picture of future care. Relational continuity is valued in primary and mental healthcare and in contexts where there are multiple caregivers, such as in inpatient nursing facilities and home health agencies.

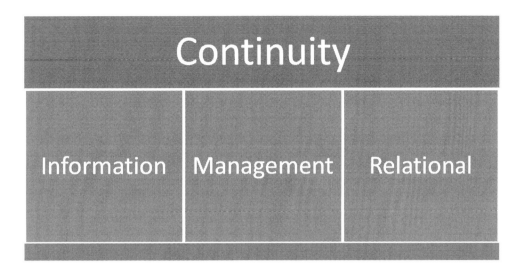

Critical Pathways and Practice Guidelines

To guide the case management process, the case manager uses critical pathways and practice guidelines, such as algorithms and a case management care plan.

Critical Pathways

Critical pathways have many other names, such as clinical pathways, integrated clinical pathways, care paths, collaborative care paths, care maps, multidisciplinary action plans, and multidisciplinary pathways of care. Regardless of the name, critical pathways are healthcare provider documents that detail the main elements of day-to-day care activities necessary for a typical patient with a specific diagnosis. These tools are created to show current practice parameters and/or recommended "best practices." Critical pathways show target lengths of stay and anticipated levels of care, and they incorporate interdisciplinary teams (McKendry, 2008).

Four Components of a Critical Pathway

- Timeline
- Identified care categories and/or activities and their interventions
- Outcome criteria, including immediate, intermediate, and long-term
- Allowance for deviations and variances

Elements of Critical Pathway Patient Care

- Assessment and monitoring
- Tests and procedures
- Care coordination and facilitation through milestones
- Consultations and referrals
- Intravenous therapy
- Medications

- Activity
- Nutrition
- Patient and family education
- Interventions and treatments, including medical, surgical, and nursing
- Pain management
- Wound care
- Physical and occupational therapy
- Safety
- Psychosocial assessment
- Outcome indicators
- Projected responses to care
- Variance identification and management
- Discharge planning (McKendry, 2008)

Algorithms

Structured in a yes/no method, algorithms are schematic models that support the use of clinical decision pathways. The decision points of an algorithm depend on specific characteristics and/or diagnostic and treatment options. These simple decision trees are useful clinical tools that do not account for all patient-related variables. Rather, they are intended to be used as guides for clinical settings, disease states, economic issues, and insurance purposes (McKendry, 2008).

Case managers use algorithms and other tools in the case management plan development process. While they are only guides, they allow the case manager to collect and report data, demonstrate the necessity of case management services, and show the full extent of case management involvement. Clinical algorithms are simple flow charts that represent the latest scientific evidence and expert consensus (McKendry, 2008).

Case Management Care Plan Development

Case management care plan development is a collaborative process where the case manager creates a "dashboard" to assist him/her in meeting the goals and responsibilities of case management and the needs of the patient, employer, health plan, and healthcare facility. An effective case management plan is a document that shows patient care needs, actions required, short- and long-term goals, time frames for the set goals, and anticipated outcomes (McKendry, 2008).

Components of Case Management Care Planning

According to the CMSA's Standards of Practice, the components of case management care planning are:

- Use of evidence-based criteria when necessary and possible

- A fiscally responsible plan that improves access, quality, and cost outcomes
- Communication with patient and family
- Communication with members of the healthcare team
- Education of the patient and family
- Contingency planning to anticipate potential complications
- Ongoing assessment and evaluation of patient progress and health
- A plan that is adaptable to changes over time and through various settings (McKendry, 2008)

Strategies for Case Management Care Plan Development

- Identification of patient-specific needs – This involves evaluating many data inputs collected during the assessment process. These include patient acuity, family and support availability, functional abilities and limitations, needed services, and available benefits.
- Collection of information regarding the type and amount of care for which the healthcare facility is responsible – This involves information necessary for care coordination and time-related issues.
- Knowledge of patient acuity – To determine the types and frequency of interventions performed, the case manager must understand patient acuity. Acuity can be determined by comorbid conditions, current illness or injury, complexity of medical needs, medication management, social support structure, and psychological/cognitive status.
- Recognition of contract-specific performance metrics – This is essential for an effective case management plan. Many organizations contract various services. Contract requirements are performance metrics, such as time frame requirements to perform services, types of services to be provided, guidelines for patient population, and anticipated outcomes from services provided.
- Assessment of quality of healthcare services – This is done through the use of quality indicators and best-practice recommendations (McKendry, 2008).

Chronic Care Model

The Chronic Care Model was created to address the deficiencies in chronic care, the aging population, and the number of patients with chronic conditions. In 1998, Improving Chronic Illness Care created this model, which summarizes the basic elements of healthcare system improvements at the patient, practice, organization, and community levels. The model can be applied to many chronic illnesses and in a variety of healthcare settings. The goal of the model is healthier patients, satisfied providers, and cost savings (Improving Chronic Illness Care, 2013).

The Chronic Care Model

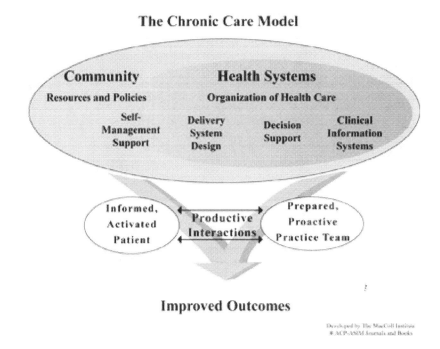

(Improving Chronic Illness Care, 2013)

A chronic condition is a disorder or disease that requires continuous adjustments by the affected individual and interactions with the healthcare system. According to Improving Chronic Illness Care (2013), more than 145 million people live with a chronic condition, and that number is expected to increase drastically by the year 2030. As a result of the aging population and the number of people with chronic conditions, many managed care and integrated healthcare delivery systems are attempting to correct deficiencies in the current management of many diseases, such as heart disease, asthma, diabetes, and depression. The deficiencies include lack of care coordination, absence of active follow-up for better outcomes, healthcare providers not adhering to established practice guidelines, and patients who are not trained and educated about their illnesses.

Elements of the Chronic Care Model

The Chronic Care Model identifies several essential elements of a healthcare system that promote high-quality chronic disease management and care:

- Community
- Healthcare system
- Self-management support
- Delivery system design
- Decision support
- Clinical information systems (Improving Chronic Illness Care, 2013)

102

Development of the Chronic Care Model

The staff at the MacColl Center for Health Care Innovation at the Group Health Research Institute developed the Chronic Care Model in the 1990s. The development process involved research of available literature regarding promising strategies for chronic illness management. In 2003, the model was updated to reflect advances in the field of chronic care through research and information from implemented healthcare systems that used the model. There were five additional elements incorporated into the Chronic Care Model: patient safety, cultural competency, care coordination, community policies, and case management (Improving Chronic Illness Care, 2013).

Delivery System Design

Improving the health of an individual with chronic conditions requires transforming a system into one that is proactive and focused on keeping that person from becoming ill. This requires determination of roles and tasks that ensures the patient receives care that is structured and planned. The delivery system design of the Chronic Care Model ensures the delivery of effective clinical care and self-management support by:

- Using planned interactions to support evidence-based care
- Defining roles and distributing tasks among team members
- Ensuring regular follow-up care
- Providing clinical case management services
- Giving care that patients need and that fits with their ethnic/cultural background (Improving Chronic Illness Care, 2013)

Self-Management Support

Patients with chronic conditions make decisions and engage in behaviors that alter their current health status, which is referred to as self-management. Disease control and improved outcomes depend on the effectiveness of the patient's self-management. Support for self-management involves acknowledging that the patient has a central role in the care, assisting with that role, and teaching home care. This involves the use of proven programs that offer basic information and strategies for living with a chronic illness. Self-management support requires a collaborative approach where patients, families, and healthcare providers all work together to identify problems, establish goals, develop treatment plans, and solve problems (Improving Chronic Illness Care, 2013).

Clinical Information Systems

Effective chronic illness care requires information systems that ensure ready access to important data regarding individual patients and populations of patients. A clinical information system enhances the care of each patient by providing timely reminders of necessary services and identifying groups of patients that require additional care. This system also facilitates the performance monitoring and quality improvement efforts of the healthcare facility. The clinical information system includes:

- Provision of timely reminders for providers and patients
- Identification of relevant subpopulations for proactive care
- Facilitation of individual patient care planning
- Information sharing with providers and patients
- Performance monitoring of the care system and practice team (Improving Chronic Illness Care, 2013)

Decision Support

Treatment decisions must be based on proven, detailed guidelines that are supported by clinical research. The guidelines must also be discussed with patients and families, so that they can understand the reason for treatments and care efforts. Healthcare providers, who make treatment decisions in collaboration with the patient, need ongoing training to remain up-to-date on the latest evidence. Guidelines should be integrated with timely reminders, standing orders, feedback, and other methods that will increase their visibility when decisions are made. Decision support involves:

- Integration of evidence-based guidelines into daily clinical practice
- Use of proven healthcare provider education methods
- Sharing of guidelines and information with patients to promote participation
- Integration of specialist expertise with primary care (Improving Chronic Illness Care, 2013)

Interdisciplinary Care Team (ICT)

An effective documentation system relies on information sharing between disciplines. Adequate communication supports the integrated team approach. The success of integrated use of interdisciplinary care plans, information technology applications, and standardized documentation allows healthcare facilities to meet the goal of high-quality patient care. The interdisciplinary care team (ICT) is made up of many healthcare providers who work together to restore health and wellness to patients. Specialization allows for in-depth exploration of issues within a discipline and means that no single provider can meet all the needs of the patient. The interdisciplinary approach has a theoretical basis that involves the entire cognitive and perceptual process for patient care (Hall & Weaver, 2001; Smith & Smith, 2005).

Healthcare teams practice along a continuum of degrees of interaction among the various members and their degrees of responsibility for patient care. Different points on the continuum are represented by the interdisciplinary team, the multidisciplinary team, and the trans-disciplinary team. While interdisciplinary team members work closely and communicate frequently to promote patient care, multidisciplinary team members work in parallel to each other with little communication. An example of a multidisciplinary team would be an orthopedic surgeon, a physiotherapist, and an occupational therapist working with a patient recovering from a fracture. The interdisciplinary team is organized around solving a common set of problems, where each team member contributes his/her skills and knowledge. With a trans-disciplinary team, team members operate at the opposite end of the continuum, professional functions overlap, and roles of individual team members are blurred (Hall & Weaver, 2001).

Collaboration among members of the interdisciplinary team requires open sharing of ideas and perspectives to solve problems. Open sharing and respect for others is necessary for this collaboration. Cost saving, time saving, and improved patient satisfaction all tend to result from innovative approaches to problem-solving (Hall & Weaver, 2001).

Chapter 5: Healthcare Reimbursement

This section covers cost-containment principles, cost-benefit analysis, the cost-effectiveness analysis method, healthcare insurance principles, reimbursement methods, managed care concepts, prospective payment systems, diagnostic-related groups, resources for the uninsured and underinsured, and utilization management.

Cost-Containment Principles

The prospected payment system promotes more efficient use of healthcare resources and encourages the study of outcomes to assess and evaluate management and economics of care. Rising healthcare costs affect the private sector through increased group health insurance premiums and changes to employee benefits. According to various reports and surveys, employers have experienced rate increases of 15-30%, and this inflation is due to a 22% increase by insurance carriers in medical benefit costs. Premium increases are the result of increases in volume and variations in health services, which have been spurred by inadequate reimbursement systems, medical technology changes, demographic changes of the aging population, care for chronically ill patients, and care for those with AIDS (Cohen & Cesta, 2005).

Cost-Containment Strategies

CMS Methods

The CMS created ambulatory patient groups (APGs), which are a reimbursement method for outpatient procedures. APGs are DRGs in the ambulatory setting that are used to reimburse the cost of providing outpatient procedures or visits. APGs do not cover physician cost elements, however. The ambulatory payment classification (APC) is a more refined reimbursement strategy that CMS implemented. APCs attempt to predict the amount and type of resources used for various ambulatory visits. Groups and payment rates are based on service categories that are similar in resource utilization and cost. Procedures that are considered "inpatient only" require more services than can be provided in the outpatient environment (Cohen & Cesta, 2005).

Another CMS initiative is the prospective payment system (PPS) for home care visits. Home health resource groups (HHRGs) must have a nursing assessment for reimbursement based on data from the Outcome and Assessment Information Set (OASIS). For inpatient and acute rehabilitation services, prospective payment uses the Inpatient Rehabilitation Facilities Patient Assessment Instrument (IRF-PAI). For skilled nursing facilities, resource utilization groups (RUGs) use the minimum data set (MDS) to differentiate nursing home patients by their levels of resource use. With this, PPS rates reimburse for ancillary, routine, and capital-related costs (Cohen & Cesta, 2005).

Reduction in Force (RIF)

Costs can be contained through a process called reduction in force (RIF). Strategies of RIF include the cutback or elimination of services that are not critical to the healthcare facility's goals regarding financial viability. One approach to RIF is outsourcing of various services, such as food, linen, housekeeping, payroll, transcription, and data processing. The use of temporary agencies for supplemental core staffing also contributes to RIF. However, RIF cost savings may be affected by hidden costs, which outstrip savings (Rundio & Wilson, 2010).

Material Management

Controlling the costs of materials (supplies and equipment) is a challenge for case managers. Economists and efficiency experts report that resources are better managed through the development and utilization of better business, care systems, and information. Competitive bidding allows the healthcare facility to obtain crucial discounts on quality products. Inventory control systems match supply and demand, decrease loss due to theft, and decrease utilization. Through pricing, frequently used items can be obtained by comparison shopping to find the most cost-effective supplies and products (Rundio & Wilson, 2010).

Clinical Variables

Numerous clinical variables have a significant effect on a patient's length of stay and healthcare costs. These include age, primary diagnosis, number of secondary diagnoses, and number of surgical procedures. Certain patient characteristics are important in judging the postoperative recovery time of patients who undergo surgical procedures, such as cholecystectomy or hysterectomy. There is a close association among age, patient dependency needs, increased time for postoperative healing, hospital-induced infections, and chronicity, which leads to a correlation between age and length of convalescent time. The following clinical variables affect length of stay:

- Urgency of emergent patient status
- Poor health status of patient
- Concomitant levels of severity of primary diagnosis
- Comorbidity and complications
- Discharge planning
- Timely social service planning
- Nursing case management model (Cohen & Cesta, 2005)

Nonclinical Variables

There are numerous nonclinical variables that affect length of stay and healthcare costs, including:

A. Day of admission – Medical admissions on Sunday have lowest average length of stay, whereas medical admissions on Friday have the highest.
B. Institutional practices – This includes those related to management, use of facility resources, and patient care delivery.
C. Interdepartmental coordination and integration of patient services – This decreased hospital length of stay (achieved by regular meetings among nursing service), laboratory personnel, and radiology personnel.
D. Increased laboratory and radiology services – This is associated with longer length of stay (Cohen & Cesta, 2005).

Cost-Benefit Analysis

Cost-benefit analysis (CBA) is the process of evaluating and assessing various scenarios to determine the relative value of an intervention when it is measured against predetermined criteria. One new approach to CBA is the Archimedes simulation model, which represents clinical, physiological, and administrative events as they occur. This model includes many aspects of care, such as personnel, care processes, facilities, protocols, disease conditions, and logistics and costs. Through bio-mathematical modeling, analysts can address complex problems without unnecessary expense and time, in contrast to traditional methods, such as observational studies and clinical trials (Rundio & Wilson, 2010).

Case managers and case management supervisors must understand and manage staff, departmental, and organizational resources and individual cases. Case managers often must conduct a CBA of a case or sections of a case. An example of this is when an insurance company refuses payment for a requested plan when it believes that a less cost-intensive solution is available (Powell, 2008).

Hard and Soft Savings

Hard savings are costs that can be saved or avoided. The case manager often facilitates hard savings, such as change in level of care, length of stay, and contracted PPO provider and such as negotiation of price of services, equipment, supplies, per diem rates, frequency of services, and duration of services. Soft savings are potential costs or charges that are less tangibly measurable than hard savings. Soft savings represent costs that are bypassed with case management intervention. Examples include avoidance of potential hospital readmissions; medical complications; acute care days; legal exposure; emergency department visits; and added costs, supplies, and equipment (Powell, 2008).

Cost-Effectiveness Analysis Method

The cost-effectiveness analysis (CEA) method is one economic process used to evaluate outcomes and costs of treatments, interventions, and delivery systems. CEA is a method for evaluating and monitoring resource costs and health outcomes of patient care, and its central function is to demonstrate the relative value of alternative interventions. This analysis produces information that can help the decision-maker evaluate the alternatives and select the most appropriate option. The CEA method is preferred among case managers for the evaluation of effectiveness of case management systems because it does not require the conversion of benefits into dollar values (Tahan, 2005c).

CEA Principles

The six principles that define the minimum acceptable standard for conducting and reporting a CEA study are:

- Principle 1: Explicit statement of analytic perspective – This typically addresses who pays certain costs (federal government, managed care organization, or commercial insurance) and who benefits from an intervention (society, patients, and family).

- Principle 2: Description of anticipated benefits – This relates to the benefits of an intervention in the case management delivery system. Examples of anticipated benefits include reduced readmission rates, patient/family satisfaction, and increased patient/family knowledge of illness and health needs.

- Principle 3: Specification of types of costs – These costs (used or considered) are derived from an analytical perspective. Examples of costs include costs of services (utilization reviews, equipment, and communication method), costs of case managers (salaries and benefits), and costs of equipment and supplies (computers, machines, and paperwork).

- Principle 4: Adjustment for differential timing – Often called discounting, adjustment for differential timing is a process that is critical when costs and benefits accrue during different time periods, generally greater than one year. With case management, discounting is crucial when CEA evaluation is performed in a time period that is greater than one year.

- Principle 5: Conduction of sensitivity analysis – This is done to test the robustness of conclusions to variations in estimates and assumptions. A sensitivity analysis investigates whether alternative assumptions explain the benefits and costs, and it reinforces the validity of various conclusions.

- Principle 6: Inclusion of efficiency summary measurement – This is the use of a cost-effectiveness (C/E) ratio to facilitate the comparison of alternative interventions. With case management, the ratio is shown using incremental cost-effectiveness terms that compare and prioritize an intervention with the next least effective or expensive one (Tahan, 2005c).

Steps of the CEA Method

The six steps identified by Arford and Allred (1995) as a method for CEA incorporation of a quality index are:

- Step 1: Identification of outcomes, benefits, and indicators – This is used to measure the effectiveness of case management systems. Examples of outcome indicators for the case management quality index include length of stay reduction, staff satisfaction, patient/family satisfaction, rate of readmissions, and rate of reimbursement denials.

- Step 2: Rating of the outcomes – The outcomes are rated in terms of importance to quality care and to effectiveness measurement. These rates are established by case management providers who apply specific research methods. A 10-point rating scale is used to rate their perception of the significance of the indicator in the outcomes of the case management system.

- Step 3: Measurement of outcomes – The outcomes are measured using appropriate methodologies as indicated by the specific outcome indicator. An example is a questionnaire used to measure patient and family satisfaction.

- Step 4: Calculation of CMQI score – The case management quality index (CMQI) score is calculated based on the unit of analysis identified in the CEA study. It can include the patient care environment.

- Step 5: Calculation of patient care costs – These costs are both direct and indirect, and they are calculated by a cost accounting system. The calculated costs reflect a relative estimate rather than 100% accurate dollar amounts. Average cost per patient is calculated by dividing the total costs per environment accrued in a specific time period by the total number of patients cared for in that environment in that same time period.

- Step 6: Calculation of cost-effectiveness ratio – The C/E ratio is a measure of case management value. A low C/E ratio is desirable because this indicates better outcomes and lower costs. A high C/E ratio is associated with lower value. Both the CMQI and C/E ratio are used to determine which practice environment is better: one with case management or one without it (Tahan, 2005c).

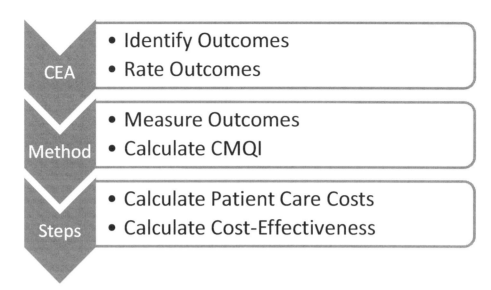

CEA
- Identify Outcomes
- Rate Outcomes

Method
- Measure Outcomes
- Calculate CMQI

Steps
- Calculate Patient Care Costs
- Calculate Cost-Effectiveness

Healthcare Insurance Principles

Key Definitions

- Capitation – This is a set amount paid to the healthcare provider on the basis of per member per year or per month, regardless of services provided.
- Co-insurance – This refers to a percentage of charges for services for which the member of the health plan must pay.
- Co-pay – This is a predetermined dollar amount for which a health plan member must pay at the time a service is rendered.
- Deductible – This refers to a fixed amount of money a health plan member must pay each year before benefits are paid by the insurance company.
- Out-of-pocket maximum – This is the maximum amount per calendar year that a health plan member pays. Co-payments, co-insurance, and deductibles all go toward this maximum (Powell & Tahan, 2010).

Commercial Payers

Commercial insurance payers are those that are not related to or sponsored by state or federal programs. Accident and health insurance includes payment for all health-related costs and often has a lifetime maximum of benefits. These programs may offer long- or short-term disability insurance. Another type of commercial payer is workers' compensation. This insurance program provides medical benefits and replaces wages for people suffering from work-related illness and/or injury (Cunningham, 2008).

The purpose of stop-loss insurance is to protect an insurance company against excessive payments. Stop-loss insurance is a form of reinsurance, which pays a percentage of bills over a certain covered amount. Stop-loss protects smaller self-funded insurance plans because the primary insurance typically covers the first

$150,000 of medical bills, and the stop-loss insurance pays around 80% of the bills over that amount (Cunningham, 2008).

Government Payers

Government insurance payers are those that are related to or sponsored by state and federal programs. Medicare was created in 1966 to finance healthcare for people over the age of 65 and those entitled to social security disability benefits. Part A covers hospitalization, and Part B covers physician services, emergency department visits, and other related services. Managed Medicare is now an option, where the member can use the service under an HMO (Cunningham, 2008).

With Medicare, the benefit period begins with patient admission to an inpatient facility and ends once the patient has been discharged from the facility for 60 days. The benefit period includes the day of admission and the day of discharge. The first 60 days require no co-insurance, but from days 61-90, the patient is responsible for a daily co-insurance charge. Hospital stay over 90 days requires the use of a lifetime reserve or another payment type. Patients often have multiple benefit periods during a one-year time period, but they must pay a deductible for each benefit period (Cunningham, 2008).

Medicaid was also created in 1966 to finance healthcare for people who are indigent, and it is jointly financed by state and federal government organizations through tax dollars. Similar to other forms of managed care, members can choose to utilize Managed Medicaid. Military insurance plans, such as Tricare and Veterans' Affairs, were created to finance healthcare for active duty and retired military personnel and their families and survivors (Cunningham, 2008).

Healthcare Reimbursement Components

   A. Limits – The limits define access to care for many insurance plans. They are related to types of services, providers the member must use, and costs and premiums.
   B. Reimbursement mechanism –This is the method applied for payment of services rendered. Examples include fee for service, case rate, capitated rate, discounted, and per diem.
   C. Risk sharing – This is the process where an HMO and healthcare provider both accept a portion of the responsibility for financial risk and reward.
   D. Credentialing – This is the review process where the insurance company approves a healthcare provider, such as a physician or nurse practitioner. Criteria for acceptance include education and training, licensure, references, board certification, and malpractice insurance (Cunningham, 2008).

Reimbursement Methods

- Fee for service – Providers are paid a set fee for each service provided, and no discounts are given.
- Discounted fee for service – Providers are paid a set fee for a specific service, but at a previously set discounted rate.
- Per diem – Organizations are paid a specific amount per day regardless of actual costs, and this is based on number of days of service and averaging costs.
- Percent of charges – Organizations are paid a fixed percentage of charges, based on the patient's bill and contractual agreements.
- DRG case rate – This is the rate of reimbursement that covers a certain category of services. This usually combines healthcare provider and facility fees.
- Carve-out services – This refers to payers and involves services that are excluded from the provider contract that can be provided through arrangement with other providers.
- Pay per performance – The organization is paid based on outcomes of specific DRGs and diseases. The outcomes can include length of stay, readmission rates, complication rates, clinical outcomes, patient/family teaching, and patient/family satisfaction.
- Global payment – Also called package pricing, this involves a predetermined payment structure that is all-inclusive and used for a specific set of related services. This is used for transplant surgeries, preoperative and postoperative care, perinatal care, and delivery services (Cunningham, 2008).

Managed Care Concepts

The term health maintenance organization (HMO) was coined in the 1970s. The advantages of these organizations include availability of and access to services through integrated group practices, creation of prepaid insurance plans, budgets for provision of services, and incentives for health maintenance and preventive services. Managed care controls escalating healthcare costs through use of various payment and cost-control measures (Gerardi, 2005).

Managed care refers to any healthcare delivery system where an outside organization influences the type of care given. The managed care organization (MCO) is the provider that intervenes to provide what is considered appropriate healthcare at an appropriate rate. Aspects of managed care include:

- Provider – The MCO allows the patient to choose from an approved list of providers and healthcare facilities.
- Prevention – Preventive services, such as immunization and well-child visits, are covered services.

- Co-payment – Most MCOs have a fixed co-payment or fee for every visit, regardless of the type of service (Gerardi, 2005).

Types of Managed Care Structures

- Health Maintenance Organizations (HMOs) – The five common models are:

  o Staff Model HMO – With this model, physicians are employed by the HMO to provide all services to health plan members.
  o Group Practice Model HMO – With this model, the HMO contracts multispecialty physician group practices to provide all services to health plan members.
  o Network Model HMO – With this model, the HMO contracts with many group practices to provide all services to health plan members.
  o Independent Practice Association (IPA) HMO – With this model, the HMO contracts an association of physicians to provide all services to health plan members.
  o Direct Contract Model HMO – With this model, the HMO contracts directly with individual physicians to provide all services to health plan members.

- Preferred Provider Organizations (PPOs) – These are entities through which health benefit plans contract to purchase healthcare services for covered beneficiaries from selected physicians. Most PPOs negotiate on the basis of discounted fee for service charges, payments based on DRGs, and all-inclusive per diem rates.

- Exclusive Provider Organizations (EPOs) – These are structured much like PPOs, but they have a limitation with provider choice. Also, EPOs are not subject to as many rigorous insurance laws as are HMOs.

- Independent Practice Associations (IPAs) – These have independent physicians or small physician group practices that contract with one or more managed healthcare organizations. An IPA can provide a large panel of providers and can accept payment on a capitated basis.

- Point of Service (POS) Plans – These contain features of both PPOs and HMOs. The physician is reimbursed through a fixed per member per month payment or other reimbursement method. With this plan, the primary care provider acts as the gatekeeper for medical services (Gerardi, 2005).

Case Management Strategies Involving Managed Care

There are numerous strategies regarding managed care that case managers must consider. These include:

- Medical management practices – This includes utilization management, case management, quality management, and disease management.
- Credentialing and re-credentialing
- Claims processing
- Information systems
- Cost containment – This includes compliance with procedures and practices in the contractual agreement between the facility and the health plan: assurance that hospital bed days are appropriate for the patient's conditions, use of demand management programs, and employment of health promotion and illness prevention strategies.
- Managed care contracts – These specify reimbursement and the denial/appeal process.
- Tracking – This includes duration of stay, length of treatment, lifetime maximum, and episode of care maximum payment.
- Compliance with NCQA standards – The NCQA is a national organization that focuses on quality of services, processes, and systems that a managed care plan delivers to members.
- Compliance with HEDIS standards – HEDIS measures are made accessible to the public, and the quality areas include cost of services, effectiveness of care, access to services, patient/family satisfaction, health plan stability, consumer health choice, credentialing, and utilization management (Gerardi, 2005).

Denials and Appeals

Appeals for a denial of urgent care services must be decided by the insurance company within 72 hours. Insurance companies have 30 days to make a decision regarding non-urgent care that the patient is waiting to receive. A patient can appeal directly to the insurance company if care is ruled medically unnecessary or is denied for some other reason. Common reasons for denial include experimental treatment, preexisting condition that is not covered, and patient ineligibility for the service (Gerardi, 2005).

Prospective Payment Systems

The Medicare prospective payment system (PPS) was initiated through Social Security amendments in 1983. Under this system, hospitals are not reimbursed under the fee for service system. Instead, they are reimbursed for various types of insurance according to DRGs. DRGs have predetermined rates of reimbursement, and the healthcare facility can keep the excess dollars if the patient does not require the total amount. However, the hospital also must incur losses for those patients who require more resources than the DRG allotment (Powell & Tahan, 2010).

PPS is in almost all care settings, such as sub-acute care, long-term care, skilled nursing care, home care, and rehabilitation.

- Ambulatory care setting – This is called the ambulatory payment classification (APC), which includes a fee schedule for bundled outpatient services.
- Rehabilitation care setting – This is called case mix groups (CMGs), which include a patient assessment instrument (PAI) for every rehabilitation patient. Based on the PAI score, the patient is placed in a CMG, which establishes the reimbursement rate for care.
- Skilled nursing facility – This is called resource utilization groups (RUGs), which involve minimum datasets for large numbers of patients to determine the RUG system. Data that establishes this system includes medical conditions, resources, and necessary services.
- Home care setting – This is called home health resource groups (HHRGs), which involve reimbursement for home care services based on a nursing assessment completed on the first home visit (Powell & Tahan, 2010).

Diagnostic-Related Groups

Diagnostic-related groups (DRGs) came about in the 1970s and were designed as a patient classification system rather than a reimbursement system. There are 25 major categories and 494 diagnoses involved with DRGs. There are numerous variables that determine the choice of DRG for a patient, such as primary diagnosis, secondary diagnosis, age, sex, complications, comorbidities, treatment procedures, discharge status, and length of stay. The DRG is scored based on its potential consumption and intensity of resources. Additionally, each DRG category has a specific acuity rating (other names for this include the relative rate and the expected length of stay) (Powell & Tahan, 2010).

Resources for the Uninsured and Underinsured

According to researchers Hadley and Associates (2008), uninsured individuals spend around $30 billion out of pocket, but receive $56 billion in uncompensated care. Government programs finance approximately 75% of this uncompensated care. This expense is the reason why expanding health insurance coverage is a major political issue. If uninsured persons were covered, medical spending would increase to $122 billion, a 5% increase in the current national health spending and 0.8% of the gross domestic product. A person is considered underinsured if he/she has health insurance, but lacks the financial resources required for medical care expenses that are out-of-pocket or in addition to that person's health plan. A person is also considered underinsured when access to health services is inhibited as the direct result of insurance benefit exclusions (Patient Advocate Foundation, 2012; Rundio & Wilson, 2010).

The Patient Advocate Foundation (PAF) provides services to Americans who have no health insurance, including applicants to Medicare and Medicaid programs. They also offer financial assistance through medical facilities and assist the uninsured patient with medications through prescription assistance programs. PAF case managers provide services to patients who are uninsured or underinsured by locating insurance coverage risk pools, guarantee issues, Consolidated Omnibus Budget Reconciliation Act (COBRA) insurance, and individual and group insurance (2013).

Utilization Management

Utilization management (UM) is a comprehensive program that is systematic and ongoing. UM review of services aims to ensure that healthcare is medically necessary and provided in the most appropriate care setting. UM review activities are conducted through onsite interfaces with members and their contracted provider or through telephonic and web services. The Utilization Review Accreditation Commission (URAC) is a nonprofit organization that does reviews and accreditations for utilization review (UR) services and programs (Lattimer & Garrett, 2008).

Types of UM Services

UM is a component of case management, which responds to one event. The three main types of UM services are:

- Prospective Review – Also called preadmission review, prospective review is completed by a representative from the healthcare provider agency to decide whether or not the admission of a patient to an inpatient facility is justified. The review occurs before services are rendered, and the reviewer decides if or not the admission is medically necessary. Most managed care organizations require a prospective review, and with this type of system, utilization of resources can be identified before the delivery of patient care.
- Concurrent Review – A concurrent review is performed while the patient is in the healthcare facility. UM reviewers conduct reviews via telephone, fax, or email. The reviewer determines level of care and communicates with the insurance company. Concurrent review involves admission review (performed within 24 hours of admission) and continued stay review (performed every two to three days).
- Retrospective Review – The retrospective review is completed after patient discharge. The reviewer goes to the facility and performs the review on the patient's medical record chart. This review is a useful tool for assessing quality control (Powell & Tahan, 2010).

The UM Review Process

1. <u>Verify patient eligibility for services</u> – This is accomplished by a customer service representative who can access the health plan's eligibility database.
2. <u>Determine covered benefit and review</u> – This is also done by a customer service representative who can access the benefit plan and check for covered services and UM review requirements.
3. <u>Collect necessary information</u> – This involves clinical information and demographic data, such as current medical situation and anticipated treatment plan, required to determine length of stay.
4. <u>Document information within a system of medical record-keeping</u> – This is done via chart, logbook, or other process.
5. <u>Select criteria and/or guidelines</u> – This is done to evaluate the requested services.
6. <u>Review clinical information against evidence-based decision support criteria and/or guidelines</u> – This is done for review determination, where the UM reviewer evaluates whether or not the case meets criteria and/or guidelines.
7. <u>Notify requesting provider and request approval</u> – This is done if the criteria and/or guidelines are met. If not met, the review will be sent for peer review by a physician advisor.
8. <u>Physician advisor reviews information and approves or disapproves the case</u> – If not approved, an offer is presented to the attending physician, called reconsideration or peer-to-peer conversation. If the request is denied, the member or provider can initiate the appeal process (Lattimer & Garrett, 2008).

UM Program Goals

- Determine medical necessity and need for services
- Ensure proper utilization of healthcare resources through continuous evaluation
- Locate patterns of underutilization, overutilization, and poor use of resources
- Promote quality care and effective outcomes

- Provide education of the UM process to healthcare providers and hospital staff
- Locate cooperation of care options for members and providers
- Identify disease management participants and case management programs (Lattimer & Garrett, 2008)

UM Review Types

- Prospective and concurrent reviews
- Precertification admissions
- Retrospective review
- Second surgical option
- Discharge planning review
- Pharmacy therapy management
- Referral review to case management (Lattimer & Garrett, 2008)

Chapter 6: Rehabilitation

This section covers rehabilitation levels of care; therapy services; work adjustment, work transition, and work hardening; workers' compensation; assessment of physical functioning; disability compensation systems; durable medical equipment and assistive technology; and job assistance.

Rehabilitation Levels of Care

Rehabilitation care and services meet the needs of people with impairments, disabilities, and handicaps. They are designed to meet specific needs, so each program is different. The general treatment components for rehabilitation programs include treating the basic disease and preventing complications, improving disability and function, providing adaptive tools, altering the environment, and teaching the patient and family how to adapt to lifestyle changes. The success of rehabilitation programs depends on the overall health of the patient, the severity of the condition, the type and degree of impairments, and the family and community support (Schoenbeck, Tahan, & Powell, 2008).

Areas of Rehabilitation Treatment

- Self-care skills – Includes activities of daily living, such as bathing, feeding, and dressing
- Mobility skills – Includes walking, transferring, and wheelchair use
- Communication skills – Includes speech, writing, and alternative methods of communication
- Cognitive skills – Includes memory, judgment, concentration, and problem-solving
- Socialization skills – Includes interacting with others in the community
- Vocational training – Includes work-related skills
- Pain management – Includes use of medicines and alternative methods of managing pain
- Psychological testing – Includes solutions for various behavioral and emotional issues
- Education – Includes training and education about coping with the illness
- Family support – Includes assistance with physical limitations, discharge planning, and financial concerns (Schoenbeck, Tahan, & Powell, 2008)

Rehabilitation Settings

- Intermediate rehabilitation facilities (IRFs) – These are free-standing hospitals or units that provide intensive rehabilitation services and care. Patients must be able to tolerate three hours of intense rehabilitation services per day, five to seven days per week. These facilities are paid under the IRF PPS.

- Comprehensive outpatient rehabilitation facilities (CORFs) – These are highly specialized outpatient facilities that provide outpatient and restorative rehabilitation services. CORFs deliver occupational therapy (OT), physical therapy (PT), and speech therapy (ST) and also prosthetic and orthotic devices and durable medical equipment (DME). Individuals who utilize CORFs must be mobile and active. Medicare Part B covers $1,500 per year on outpatient PT/OT services.

- Skilled nursing facilities (SNFs) – Sub-acute rehabilitation is a cost-effective means of service provision for those patients who no longer require intensive hospital care, but have a need for rehabilitation. The three categories of care for these services include short-term, short-term complex medical, and long-term chronic (Schoenbeck, Tahan, & Powell, 2008).

Therapy Services

In many skilled nursing facilities, 30% of the charges are for rehabilitation services. Because of the need for these services, PPSs have made changes in the rehabilitation area. RUGs II categories include reimbursement for the minutes of therapy provided to the patient. However, this does not include the time required for the initial evaluation, development of treatment goals, and creation of the plan of care. Actual minutes of therapy are significant for the RUGs III level, so many therapists carry stopwatches to document accuracy in minutes. The two highest therapy levels are ultra-high level, which is a minimum of 720 minutes of therapy per week, and very high level, which is a minimum of 500 minutes of therapy per week (Powell & Tahan, 2010).

Medicare assists with payment for medically necessary outpatient OT, PT, and ST services if the physician or therapist sets up the plan and if the physician periodically reviews that plan for patient progression and additional need for services. OT, PT, and ST services must be obtained from a Medicare-participating outpatient provider, such as a home health agency, hospital-based clinic, or comprehensive rehabilitation center. Respiratory therapy is included in the per diem Medicare reimbursement rate. The RUGs III grouping considers respiratory therapy in extensive services, clinically complex patients, and special care (Powell & Tahan, 2010).

Work Adjustment, Work Transition, and Work Hardening

Workforce management involves work adjustment, work transition, and work hardening. The concept of workforce management involves all aspects of occupational disability and proactive health and safety information and training and of non-occupational lost-time cases and effective return-to-work status. Workforce management includes benefit plan design; demographics of the employer's worker populations; health and productivity programs; and integration of benefit programs, such as integrated disability management and occupational case management (Provine & Vierling, 2008).

Work Adjustment

The Worker Adjustment and Retraining Notification (WARN) Act offers protection to workers, their families, and their communities by requiring employers to give notice 60 days in advance of plant closing and mass layoffs. Enacted in 1988, this law requires employers to also give notice to workers' representatives (labor unions), to the state dislocated worker unit, and to the appropriate section of the local government. Employers covered by WARN include: those who have 100 or more employees who have worked for more than six months in the last 12 months and those who work an average of 20 hours or more per week. Federal, state, and local government entities that provide public services are not covered. Covered employees include hourly and salaried workers and supervisory staff (U.S. Department of Labor, 2013).

WARN Provisions

- Plant closing – A covered employer must give notice if an employment site will be shut down and will result in employment loss for 50 or more employees during a 30-day period.

- Mass layoff – A covered employer must give notice if there is to be a mass layoff, which does not cause the plant to close, but rather will result in employment loss at the employment site for 500 or more employees during a 30-day period. This also applies for 50-499 employees if they constitute at least 33% of the employer's active workforce.

- Threshold requirements – A covered employer must give notice if the number of employment losses during a 30-day period do not meet the threshold requirements for a plant closing or mass layoff, but the number of losses for two or more groups of workers reaches the threshold level during a 90-day period of either a plant closing or a mass layoff. WARN threshold levels will consist of job losses within any 90-day period unless the employer shows that these losses are the result of separate and distinct causes and/or actions.

- Sale of business – In each situation, the employer must be responsible for giving notice. If the sale of a business results in a covered plant closing or mass layoff, employees must receive at least a 60-day notice. The buyer must provide notice of plant closing or mass layoff that occurs after the time of sale (U.S. Department of Labor).

Employment Loss

Employment loss means an employment termination that occurs due to something other than voluntary departure, retirement, or discharge for cause. This includes a layoff that exceeds six months or a reduction in an employee's hours of work of more than 50% in each month of any six-month period. The exception to this is an employee who refuses a transfer to another worksite within reasonable commuting distance. The exemption to this portion of the WARN law is that an employer does not need to give notice if a plant closing occurs at a temporary facility or if the closing or layoff is the result of the completion of a specified project.

Notification Period

There are three exceptions to which required parties must be given notice 60 days or more before a closing or layoff: faltering company, unforeseeable business circumstances, and natural disaster. All notices must be in writing and distributed through a reasonable method of delivery so that concerned parties receive notice 60 days before closing or layoff. Notice must also be specific. Enforcement of WARN requirements is through U.S. district courts (U.S. Department of Labor, 2013).

Work Transition

Work transition programs, also called transitional work duty (TWD) programs, are progressive and time-limited, focusing on getting the disabled or injured employee back to work with necessary restrictions. Work transition allows the injured worker to perform productive duties at the workplace while under the care of rehabilitation professionals. Work transition programs use structured protocols that focus on return-to-work. Specific restrictions and modifications may include: vocational abilities to maximize recovery, alternate work functions and duties, and tailored work duties to accommodate the employee's medical limitations (Provine & Vierling, 2008).

TWD programs cover disabling conditions insured under workers' compensation, and a TWD assignment must be documented by a transitional work plan, written for a certain period of time. Average plans are 90 calendar days. Eligible employees include those with temporary partial disabilities, if their recovery is considered short-term. TWD programs do not cover employees with permanent disabilities (Provine & Vierling, 2008).

Work Hardening

Work hardening is an interdisciplinary, job-specific concept that involves activity with the goal of return-to-work, and it provides a transition between acute care and successful return-to-work. Work-hardening programs are individualized and use real or simulated work tasks and conditioning exercises that are based on the injured person's measured tolerances (Washington State Department of Labor & Industries, 2013).

Components of a Work-Hardening Program

- Identification of strength and endurance of the patient in relation to the return-to-work goal

- Use of equipment and methods that quantify and measure conditioning and strength levels, such as ergometers, dynamometers, treadmills, and measured walking tolerances
- Simulation of critical work demands of the worker in a progressive manner
- Education regarding body mechanics, safety and injury prevention, and work pacing
- Assessment of job modification needs, such as added equipment, changes in the ergonomics of the worksite, and changes in work position
- An individualized written plan that specifies measurable goals, how to reach those goals, the time needed to accomplish those goals, and the expected outcomes
- A safe work environment that is adequate for the vocational goal and a designated work-hardening area separate from treatment of medical patients (Washington State Department of Labor & Industries, 2013)

Example Criteria for Admission into a Work-Hardening Program

- Physical recovery sufficient to permit progressive reactivation and participation for a minimum of four hours per day for three to five days per week
- A defined return-to-work goal or documented on-the-job training
- Worker ability to benefit from the program, documented by a screening review used to determine the likelihood of success
- Worker must be no more than two years past date of injury (Washington State Department of Labor & Industries, 2013)

Example Criteria for Discharge from a Work-Hardening Program

- Worker has reached the goals of the plan
- Worker has not participated, as he/she should have, in the plan
- Goals were discovered to not be feasible, or a previously unknown medical problem was found (Washington State Department of Labor & Industries, 2013)

Workers' Compensation

Workers' compensation laws were developed by federal statute in 1908, but they are enforced at the state level. New York was the first state to enact the law in response to a factory fire that killed 146 women. In 1950, Mississippi became the last state to enact the law. Workers' compensation varies from state to state, but it is designed to provide medical and compensatory benefits to employees who are hurt or injured on the job. The three types of benefits provided under these state laws are indemnity cash benefits for lost wages, survivors' death benefits, and reimbursement for necessary medical expenses (Powell & Tahan, 2010).

Workers' compensation claims often involve repetitive motion injuries, trauma, and neuromuscular impairment. Many employees submit claims for soft tissue injuries with nonspecific diagnoses. These claims lack objective clinical findings and challenge the utilization review process. Common diagnoses include muscle sprains and strains, low back pain, wrist pain, and neck pain. These problems do not show up on x-rays and diagnostic scans, which affect levels of care and insurance coverage (Powell & Tahan, 2010).

Goals of Workers' Compensation Programs

- Provide injured or ill workers with prompt medical care and wage replacement for themselves, their dependents, and/or their survivors
- Establish a primary remedy for workplace injuries to decrease or eliminate legal expenses
- Provide a system for workers' compensation benefits and services delivery
- Relieve the private and public sectors of financial demands regarding medical services
- Promote workplace safety and accident prevention (Powell & Tahan, 2010)

The Case Manager's Role in Workers' Compensation

Workers' compensation insurance carriers and self-insured employers desire to decrease costs of claims submitted. Many strategies for keeping claim costs low include loss control; safety and health programs; risk management; and managed care arrangements, such as medical case management. The case manager must use various tools to lower medical costs, promote best medical and claim outcomes, maintain a stable workforce, and improve communication. Case managers assist the injured employee, the employer, the provider, the insurance carrier, and the third-party administrator (TPA) in understanding the impact of injury, illness, disability, and the workers' compensation system on medical care (DiBenedetto, 2008).

Workers' Compensation Case Management

Case management practices are applied in the workers' compensation industry setting. Medical case management processes include:

- Case identification and targeting – Many "lost time" or "indemnity" claims are referred for case management.
- Evaluation and assessment – Case managers must assess the injured or ill worker's needs through medical record and claim review; direct contact with the worker, healthcare providers, and employer; and evaluation of the treatment plan and care setting.
- Problem identification, planning, and solving – This involves recognition of problems that result from work-related injury or illness and their ramifications.
- Coordination of healthcare providers – There are usually multiple healthcare providers working with the patient. The case manager needs to monitor

healthcare progress, make necessary recommendations, and assist the worker in receiving the most effective care available.

- Utilization review – The case manager must practice utilization review of laws that regulate healthcare service selection.
- Precertification and preauthorization – With workers' compensation, precertification and preauthorization of procedures, equipment, and services is often mandatory.
- Negotiation and contracting – The case manager must be aware of "usual and customary" costs listed in various databases before negotiating prices with healthcare providers.
- Reporting – Reporting of all assessment, planning, intervention, and outcome activities is done to document the value of case management services and to assist the injured or ill worker toward maximum medical improvement (DiBenedetto, 2008).

Assessment of Physical Functioning

Function, disability, and impairment are all words related to physical mobility and capability. There are several ways to measure physical functioning, including the functional capacity evaluation (FCE), the Instrumental Activities of Daily Living (IADL) tool, and the Barthel Index of Activities of Daily Living tool.

Functional Capacity Evaluation

The functional capacity evaluation (FCE) is an instrument that reliably measures the functional physical ability of a person to perform work-related tasks. Three terms used to assess reliability are intra-rater reliability, test-retest reliability, and inter-rater reliability. The FCE instrument must also be valid, implying that the test measures what it claims to measure. An FCE can determine fitness to work after an extended period of medical leave, help identify changes to the employee's workload, and identify ergonomic measures that the employer must take to accommodate an employee with a medical condition or disability (Chen, 2007).

The Instrumental Activities of Daily Living (IADL) Tool

The Instrumental Activities of Daily Living (IADL) tool is used to evaluate patients with early-stage disease, to assess the level of the disease, and to determine the patient's ability to perform self-care tasks. The IADL scale assesses the functional impact of cognitive, emotional, and physical impairments. The Instrumental Activities of Daily Living tool assesses:

- Shopping
- Telephone use
- Bill paying
- Budgeting

- Food preparation
- Housekeeping
- Laundry
- Transportation
- Medication use (Lawton & Brody, 1969)

The Barthel Index of Activities of Daily Living Tool

The Barthel Index of Activities of Daily Living tool was developed in 1965 and later modified. This tool measures functional disability by quantification of 10 activities of patient performance. The scoring system uses five-point increments with a maximum score of 100, indicating that the patient is fully independent in physical functioning. The Barthel Index of Activities of Daily Living tool assesses:

- Bathing
- Toileting
- Grooming
- Stair climbing
- Feeding
- Mobility
- Personal grooming
- Urinary and fecal control
- Transferring
- Ambulatory/wheelchair status (Mahoney & Barthel, 1965)

Disability Compensation Systems

Disability is any physical or neurological deviation in a person's makeup that results in a diminished function and reduced ability to engage in substantial gainful activity. Disability case management is the process of managing diseases to return the disabled person to productive work and employment. It also provides immediate interventions once an illness or injury has occurred. Disability management programs involve coordinated access to benefit plans and services that assist a person with a disability. These include:

- Workers' compensation
- Sick leave
- Healthcare benefits
- State disability
- Salary continuation, pension, and retirement plans
- Medical leaves of absence
- Union plans
- Paid time off (PTO)
- Social Security Disability (Provine & Vierling, 2008)

Disability Case Management

Disability case management is a process that follows various functions and activities. These include: performing individual case analysis and benefits assessment, reviewing disability case management intervention protocols, collaborating with stakeholders, performing job analyses, developing return-to-work plans, implementing interventions, coordinating benefits and services, monitoring progress, and managing a caseload of clients. Disability managers are part of an interdisciplinary team involved in productivity improvement, benefit practice, and wellness programs (Provine & Vierling, 2008).

Three Practice Domains for Disability Management Specialists

The Certification of Disability Management Specialists Commission (CDMSC) identifies three specific practice domains for disability management specialists. These are:

- Disability case management – This involves specific tasks and knowledge to perform various tasks related to working with people who are injured, are ill, or have a disability.
- Disability prevention and workplace intervention – This brings together organizational and individual practice to identify how tasks and duties within disability management have formed and evolved, with responsibility to the individual and programs.
- Program development, management, and evaluation – This combines the administrative and managerial tasks that are the responsibility of the disability manager (Provine & Vierling, 2008).

Occupational Health Case Management

Occupational health nursing is the specialty practice that delivers and provides healthcare and safety programs and services to workers, workers' families, worker populations, and community groups. Occupational health case management prevents fragmented care and recovery issues by facilitating appropriate return-to-work or modified work capacity. This process involves the goal of returning the worker to his/her pre-illness or pre-injury function or to the highest level of functioning possible (Provine & Vierling, 2008).

Role of Occupational Health Case Managers

Occupational health case managers provide services that rely on the nature of the business setting, the philosophy of the case management program, and the expectations of the employer. In collaboration with other healthcare providers, these case managers coordinate the proactive efforts of the interdisciplinary team to facilitate the patient's healthcare services from the illness or injury onset to the end of case management services. Occupational health case managers serve as gatekeepers for rehabilitation, health services, and case management issues (Provine & Vierling, 2008).

Durable Medical Equipment, Assistive Technology, and Ergonomics

There are many services available through each state's vocational rehabilitation system, and they can play a key role in assisting people with disabilities in the workplace. Assistive technology (AT) can significantly enhance employment options for many individuals with disabilities. Also, durable medical equipment (DME) assists disabled and elderly people in the home setting. The Rehabilitation Act was first initiated in 1973, giving states money to provide vocational rehabilitation services to people with disabilities (Hagar, 2013).

Durable Medical Equipment (DME)

Durable medical equipment (DME) is the term used to describe any assistive device or piece of equipment or technology that is used in the patient's home or community setting or in an institution that meets the requirements of the insurance company. DME can be furnished on a rental basis or purchased. For Medicare to cover DME, it must be approved by the insurance company and ordered by one of the patient's physicians. Medicare will cover DME only if the physician or supplier is enrolled in the Medicare program. When the supplier is not enrolled with federal Medicare services, Medicare cannot limit how much the supplier charges for the DME (Powell & Tahan, 2010).

DME Categories

DME is often called home medical equipment (HME) and is categorized into four groups:

- Basic mobility aids – Includes canes, crutches, and walkers
- Assistive devices for independence with ADLs – Includes shower chairs, hand rails, kitchen equipment, wound care supplies, and ostomy care supplies
- Mobility aids – Includes electric beds and wheelchairs
- High-technology equipment – Includes ventilators, IV pumps, infusion pumps, apnea/sleep monitors, and special electric beds (Powell & Tahan, 2010)

Medicare DME Costs

The amount the Medicare beneficiary pays for DME is based on what type of equipment is needed. After paying a $131 Medicare Part B deductible, the beneficiary may still have to pay for 20% co-insurance. The equipment must also be purchased from a Medicare-participating supplier. CMS will allow DME to be delivered two days before patient discharge from the hospital, so the equipment will be there when the patient goes home. Case managers should document why the DME is delivered early to avoid alerting CMS. No bills can be rendered for DME before the date of patient discharge from the facility to the home. Some special requirements exist for home oxygen (Powell & Tahan, 2010).

Assistive Technology

The Rehabilitation Act uses the definitions of assistive technology (AT) devices and services contained in the Assistive Technology for Individuals with Disabilities Act (also called the "AT Act"). The term "assistive technology device" means any item, product system, or piece of equipment, whether acquired commercially off the shelf, customized, or modified, that is used to increase, maintain, and/or improve functional capabilities of persons with disabilities. The term "assistive technology service" means any service that directly assists an individual with a disability in the selection, acquisition, or use of an assistive technology device. This includes:

- Evaluation of the needs of a person with a disability, including a functional capacity evaluation of the person's customary environment
- Purchasing, leasing, or otherwise providing for the acquisition of assistive technology devices by individuals with disabilities
- Selecting, fitting, designing, customizing, applying, adapting, maintaining, repairing, or replacing assistive technology devices
- Coordination and use of other therapies, interventions, or services with assistive technology devices, such as those associated with existing rehabilitation and education and rehabilitation programs and plans
- Training or technical assistance for a person with disabilities or the family members, guardians, advocates, or authorized representatives of such a person
- Training or technical assistance for professionals, employers, or people who provide services to, employ, or are otherwise substantially involved in major life functions of people with disabilities (Hagar, 2013)

The AT Act was originally called the Technology-Related Assistance for Individuals with Disabilities Act of 1988. This act indicates the broad range of AT devices that were contemplated by the developing committee. The AT Act provides maximum flexibility to enable the states to address the numerous and varying needs of people with all categories of disabilities and to emphasize that adaptations to equipment are included under the definition, as are low- and high-technology items and software (Hagar, 2013).

In Title I of the Rehabilitation Act, the availability of AT devices and services are included in the definition of "rehabilitation technology." Rehabilitation technology is the systematic application of technologies, scientific principles, and engineering methodologies to meet the needs of and address the barriers confronted by persons with disabilities in areas of employment, transportation, education, rehabilitation, recreation, and independent living. Additionally, the term includes AT devices, AT services, and rehabilitation engineering (Hagar, 2013).

Ergonomics

Ergonomics is a scientific discipline that is concerned with the interactions among humans and other elements of a system. Also called human factors engineering, human engineering, and biotechnology, it is the applied science of equipment design, which is intended to increase productivity by reducing operator discomfort and fatigue. This method is used to prevent injury associated with repetitive motions, forceful movements, motions, or grips on objects and with unchanging and/or poor postures (Provine & Vierling, 2008).

Ergonomics applies theory principles, data, and methods to environmental design, including work environments. This is done to optimize overall system performance and human well-being. Assistive technology is an umbrella term that includes adaptive, rehabilitative, and assistive devices for people with disabilities. This concept involves any item, product system, or piece of equipment that is used to develop, maintain, and/or improve functional capabilities in persons with disabilities (Provine & Vierling, 2008).

Job Assistance

The Job Accommodation Network (JAN) is a service provided by the Office of Disability Employment Policy of the U.S. Department of Labor. The mission of JAN is to encourage and assist with the employment and retention of workers with disabilities by providing information regarding job accommodations to employers, employment providers, people with disabilities, and other interested parties. In a recent survey of employers that used the JAN network, more than half of the accommodations necessary for both employers and job applicants with disabilities involve no additional cost (Provine & Vierling, 2008).

In 1999, Congress passed the Ticket to Work and Work Incentive Improvement Act (TWWIIA). This legislation gives people with disabilities both incentive and the means to seek employment. Previously, the threat of losing healthcare coverage was a barrier for many with a disability, and around 70% of those people are unemployed. The TWWIIA addresses the issues related to loss of healthcare coverage by letting states extend coverage under Medicaid for many people with disabilities. The workers are allowed to either purchase the Medicaid coverage or extend their eligibility for the program. Also, this law gives beneficiaries Medicare hospital coverage for four and a half years when they return to work (Provine & Vierling, 2008).

Test Your Knowledge

Case Management Concepts (25%)

1. Which concept is systems-oriented and involves the management of various benefits of health insurance plans?
    A. Case management
    B. Managed care
    C. Care management
    D. Care Coordination

2. Which of the following is NOT one of the principles of case management practice?
    A. Focus on patient and family
    B. Negotiating, procuring, and coordinating services and resources
    C. Use of the clinical reasoning process
    D. Insurance-based

3. What diagnostic category constitutes a condition of a target patient population that meets patient selection criteria for case management?
    A. Acute injury or illness
    B. Chronic injury or illness
    C. Multiple diagnoses
    D. None of the above
    E. All of the above

4. Of the following patients, which one would NOT be considered for case management services?
    A. 15-year-old female with a urinary tract infection
    B. 88-year-old 100-pound female who has suffered a hip fracture
    C. 42-year-old man who is on the list for a kidney transplant
    D. 22-year-old man who was recently diagnosed with schizophrenia

5. Why do the roles and responsibilities of the case manager vary?
    A. Because the settings where care is provided vary
    B. Because the patient population served varies
    C. Because the case mix of patients varies
    D. All of the above
    E. None of the above

6. Within the domain of case management related to case finding and intake, which of the following tasks would you expect to perform?
    A. Facilitating and coordinating care activities
    B. Obtaining informed consent for services
    C. Reviewing and modifying healthcare services
    D. Data collecting, analyzing, and reporting

7. All of the following are components of the utilization management domain of case management EXCEPT:
    A. Evaluation of appropriate level of care
    B. Communication with payers and other healthcare providers
    C. Allocation of resources based on insurance requests
    D. Management of reimbursement appeals and denials

8. The evaluation and case closure domain of case management involves which of the following concepts?
    A. Serving as patient and family advocate
    B. Reporting termination of services to stakeholders
    C. Managing reimbursement appeals and denials
    D. Assessing a patient's support network

9. Which of the following is NOT a component of the vocational issues domain of case management?
    A. Identification of need for changes in the home environment
    B. Elimination of access barriers
    C. Review of patient condition for appropriateness of hospitalization
    D. Arrangement for vocational assessment and services

10. Which of the following is one purpose of case management practice?
    A. To minimize efficiency of valuable and available resource usage
    B. To promote informed decision-making by the patient and others by interjecting objectivity and information
    C. To work with the insurance company to implement a plan of care that meets the patient's needs
    D. To make the healthcare delivery system more costly

11. The nurse case manager identifies acute care needs and discharge requirements in addition to developing the treatment plan along with members of an interdisciplinary team. Which model does the case manager use?
    A. Primary Nurse Case Management Model
    B. Acute Care Case Management Model
    C. Leveled Practice Model
    D. Emergency Department Case Management Model

12. Which of the following professional communication skills is used to facilitate communication with interdisciplinary team members?
    A. Asking questions that challenge someone's ideas
    B. Providing advice when it is needed
    C. Interpreting the statements of a person to improve idea flow
    D. Reacting to facts rather than to feelings

13. Regarding the Acute Care Case Management Model, which of the five methods is involved when the case manager follows patients from admission to discharge?
    A. Unit-based
    B. Complete-based
    C. Practice-based
    D. Disease-based

14. With which model does the nurse case manager act as a liaison between care levels to assist the patient during the convalescent period by assessing his/her condition and determining appropriate services?
    A. Rehabilitation Case Management Model
    B. Community-Based Case Management Model
    C. Skilled Nursing Facility Case Management Model
    D. Independent/Private Case Management Model

15. Which of the following is NOT an example of a population served under the Community-Based Case Management Model?
    A. Homeless families
    B. Substance abuse patients
    C. Mental health patients
    D. Geriatric patients
    E. None of the above

16. Which of the following are benefits of working as an independent case manager under the Independent/Private Case Management Model?
    A. Stable income and working with all types of patients
    B. Flexibility and autonomy in decision-making
    C. Interdisciplinary team assistance with planning
    D. Help with decision-making

17. Which value is calculated by multiplying the relative weight and the facility's base rate?
    A. Case mix index
    B. Caseload matrix
    C. Hospital payment
    D. None of the above

18. Which of the following affects the case load index?
    A. Severity of illness
    B. Need for intervention
    C. Treatment difficulty
    D. Presence of complications and/or comorbidities
    E. All of the above

19. Which of the following is a true statement concerning major diagnostic categories (MDCs)?
    A. DRGs are not separated by MDCs.
    B. The number of DRGs in each MDC ranges from 1 to 10.
    C. MDCs are grouped according to anatomical and pathophysiological sections.
    D. MDCs are categorized as either acute or chronic.

20. Which calculation is used to identify variables in various settings that affect caseloads?
    A. Case management (CM) outcomes
    B. Major diagnostic categories (MDCs)
    C. Caseload matrix
    D. Case mix index (CMI)

21. Which indicator dictates the complexity and types of services provided by a healthcare facility?
    A. Severity of illness
    B. Prognosis
    C. Number of patients
    D. Both A and B

22. The severity of illness indicator that represents an illness that occurred within one week is:
    A. Acute/sudden onset
    B. Recent onset
    C. New onset
    D. Newly discovered

23. As _____ level rises, more nurses are needed to provide adequate and safe care.
    A. Acuity
    B. Severity of illness
    C. Intensity of service
    D. Discharge screen

24. Of the following, which is NOT an indicator of a severity of illness criteria?
    A. Oral temperature of 104° Fahrenheit
    B. Sustained pulse of greater than 100 bpm
    C. Respiratory rate greater than 22 with pulse oximeter less than 88% on room air
    D. Diastolic blood pressure greater than 120 or less than 40 mmHg

25. Discharge screens indicate:
    A. If the patient is clinically ready for discharge
    B. If the patient is clinically ready for transfer
    C. If the patient is stable enough for this process
    D. All of the above
    E. None of the above

26. With InterQual's review process, the admission review is:
    A. Initiated before patient admission to the healthcare facility
    B. Usually the initial chart review, done within 24 hours of admission
    C. Done throughout the hospitalization, typically every three days
    D. Initiated when the patient is ready for discharge or transfer

27. Which of the following is NOT one of the four types of review involved in InterQual's review process?
    A. Preadmission
    B. Admission
    C. Case closure
    D. Discharge

28. The type of conflict that occurs between the self and another person is:
    A. Intrapersonal
    B. Interpersonal
    C. Intragroup
    D. Intergroup

29. Coaching and educating healthcare providers and nurses regarding conflict can be accomplished by/through:
    A. Role-playing exercises, staff meetings, educational videos, and effective communication
    B. Procedures and processes for identification of potential common conflicts
    C. Engaging in dialogues that address conflict in order to create a healthy work environment
    D. Careful consideration of the objectives that led to the conflict

30. When communication does not resolve an ethical problem or conflict among the concerned parties, the case manager should consult or meet with the:
    A. Attending physician
    B. Ethics committee
    C. Nurse manager
    D. Patient's family

31. Which case management model involves joint decision-making among numerous parties where these persons have collective responsibility for outcomes and bring positive outcomes, such as reduced cost with improved quality of care and increased patient and staff satisfaction?
    A. Collaborative Case Management Model
    B. Medical-Social Case Management Model
    C. Home Health Case Management Model
    D. Palliative Care Case Management Model

32. Which case management model focuses on the long-term care patient who is at risk for hospitalization; involves resource utilization of services that are not usually covered by health insurance, but are necessary to maintain the patient in the home setting; and includes care planning, assessment, coordination, and care monitoring processes?
    A. Collaborative Case Management Model
    B. Medical-Social Case Management Model
    C. Home Health Case Management Model
    D. Palliative Care Case Management Model

33. Which case management model is often used in clinical practices, such as identifying patients with diabetes and encouraging them to attend education classes or when distributing materials to women who need Pap smears?
    A. Admission Office Case Management Model
    B. Large Case Management Model
    C. Disease Management Model
    D. Insurance Case Management Model

34. What is the proper sequence for the stages of the case management process?
    A. Case selection, problem identification, case plan development and coordination, case plan reassessment and reevaluation, case plan implementation, case plan evaluation, case closure
    B. Case plan development and coordination, problem identification, case plan reassessment and reevaluation, case plan evaluation, case plan implementation, case selection, case closure
    C. Case selection, problem identification, case plan development and coordination, case plan implementation, case plan evaluation, case plan reassessment and reevaluation, case closure
    D. Case selection, problem identification, case plan evaluation, case plan development and coordination, case plan implementation, case plan reassessment and reevaluation, case closure

35. The case manager is called to assess a patient with anorexia nervosa. During the stage of case selection, which type of indicator is this?
    A. General indicator
    B. Psychosocial indicator
    C. Socioeconomic indicator
    D. None of the above

36. Which of the following patients would be appropriate for case management due to certain socioeconomic indicators in the case selection process?
    A. 22-year-old college student with a first degree burn who lives in the town where you work
    B. 65-year-old chief executive officer who has heartburn and resides one mile from the hospital where you work
    C. 32-year-old woman who lives in a rural part of a neighboring state ,
    D. 54-year-old asthmatic Asian woman who was born in America and resides nearby

37. Which of the five categories of healthcare data is concerned with a particular patient, device, or thing?
    A. Subgroup data
    B. Historical data ,
    C. Workflow management data
    D. Encounter patient data

38. Outcome measures in case management should demonstrate that:
    A. The case manager has four key functions.
    B. Effective performance of these four functions positively impacts outcomes.
    C. Both A and B
    D. Neither A nor B

39. What type of database is used by nurse managers and analysts for population-based management and is trended, comparative, and aggregate?
    A. Data repository
    B. Data warehouse
    C. Data validity
    D. Data reliability

40. A 72-year-old Italian woman who lives with her daughter is brought into the emergency department. The daughter does most of the talking for the patient. When the daughter leaves, a staff nurse asks the patient if she would like a glass of water. The lady smiles back at the nurse and looks down at her hands. What should the nurse case manager consider?
    A. The patient is probably on a mind-altering substance.
    B. The patient has a language barrier or hearing impairment.
    C. The patient is noncompliant.
    D. The patient has had a stroke.

41. A case manager is conducting research concerning the gender of a patient population. Male sex is number one (1), and female sex is number two (2). What level of measurement and data type is gender?
    A. Nominal level of measurement; nonparametric data type
    B. Ordinal level of measurement; nonparametric data type
    C. Interval level of measurement; parametric data type
    D. Ratio level of measurement; parametric data type

42. A preexisting condition that prolongs the length of stay by at least one day in 75% of cases is a:
    A. Complication
    B. Mortality
    C. Comorbidity
    D. DRG relative weight

43. A patient that has a disability related to mobility would have which type of Quality of Life (QOL) indicator?
    A. Social functioning
    B. Psychological functioning
    C. General well-being
    D. Physical functioning

44. Which healthcare facility concept focuses on identifying potential risk areas and interventions that will improve patient safety while preventing adverse events or unfortunate incidents?
    A. Quality improvement
    B. Performance improvement
    C. Quality assurance
    D. Risk management

45. During an interview with a newly admitted patient, which type of patient response gives the case manager the most useful information?
    A. Silence
    B. Non-verbal response
    C. Verbal response
    D. Both non-verbal and verbal responses

Principles of Practice (15%)

1. The organizations that offer accreditation programs for case management programs include all of the following EXCEPT:
   A. Commission on Accreditation of Rehabilitation Facilities (CARF)
   B. Utilization Review Accreditation Commission (URAC)
   C. Accreditation Commission for Health Care (ACHC)
   D. American Nurses Association (ANA)

2. The accreditation process involves:
   A. A review of documentation of employee and staff vaccine records
   B. A telephone evaluation to assess organizational function
   C. An assessment of the case mix index
   D. A review of documentation of policies and procedures

3. A 44-year-old man insists that his pain medicine is not working. He calls the nurse case manager and asks her to contact the physician for another medication. Due to past issues with this patient, the nurse believes the patient is noncompliant and refuses to advocate for him. Which ethical principle is involved in this situation?
   A. Autonomy
   B. Non-maleficence
   C. Beneficence
   D. Justice

4. What ethical conflicts are related to individuals of the healthcare facility and pertain to a hospital or facility's behaviors?
   A. Organizational ethical conflicts
   B. Physician ethical conflicts
   C. Nurse ethical conflicts
   D. Clinical ethical conflicts

5. Which item in the Code of Professional Conduct for Case Managers describes the role of the case manager in legal compliance, client identity, electronic recordings, disclosure, storage, disposal, and reporting?
   A. Advocacy
   B. Case manager and patient relationship
   C. Confidentiality, privacy, and record-keeping
   D. Research

6. The Employee Retirement Income Security Act (ERISA):
   A. Added many strategies that support human capital management.
   B. Involves the regulation of pension plans
   C. Is a national managed care demonstration program that provides and finances long-term care for the elderly
   D. Entitles eligible employees of certain covered employers to take unpaid, job-protected leave for specified medical and family reasons with continuation of group health insurance coverage

7. The FMLA applies only to certain employers. These include:
    A. Private-sector employer with 50 or more employees in 20 or more workweeks in the current or preceding calendar year, including a successor or joint employer in interest to a covered employer
    B. Public agency, including local, state, or federal agencies, regardless of the number of employees
    C. Public or private elementary or secondary schools, regardless of the number of employees
    D. All of the above

8. Comprehensive healthcare reform in the U.S. was not enacted by Congress until:
    A. 1993
    B. 1995
    C. 2005
    D. 2010

9. Which act ensures that qualified individuals with disabilities enjoy the same employment opportunities as those without any physical or mental disability?
    A. Family and Medical Leave Act (FMLA)
    B. Americans with Disabilities Act (ADA)
    C. Equal Pay Act of 1963
    D. Rehabilitation Act of 1973

10. Which of the following represents "reasonable accommodation" under the Americans with Disabilities Act?
    A. To the job application process that allow a qualified individual with a disability to be considered for a certain position
    B. To the work environment circumstances, or manner under which the position is held, that allow a qualified person with a disability to perform the necessary work functions
    C. That enable an employee with a disability to profit from the same privileges and benefits as those without disabilities
    D. All of the above

11. Which of the following provides federal protection for individually identifiable healthcare information held by covered facilities and their business associates?
    A. The HIPAA Privacy Rule
    B. The HIPAA Security Rule
    C. The HIPAA Availability Rule
    D. The HIPAA Integrity Rule

12. Which of the following is a true statement?
    A. With the Fair Labor Standards Act, an employee who becomes ill or who is injured on the job or from a condition caused by the worksite is compensated for that incident.
    B. Workers' compensation laws are federal statutes, which establish liability of employers for injuries or illnesses to or of workers on the job due to the employment.
    C. The U.S. Department of Labor is the federal department that governs OSHA.
    D. The Occupational Safety and Health Act (OSHA) of 1970 is enforced by the Equal Employment Opportunity Commission (EEOC).

13. According to OSHA, employers with _____ or more employees must keep records of work-related illnesses and injuries.
    A. 10
    B. 11
    C. 12
    D. 20

14. Failure to provide reasonable care based on expertise and appropriate standards is an example of:
    A. Negligence
    B. Malpractice
    C. Laziness
    D. Poor supervision

15. A qualified handicapped person under the Rehabilitation Act of 1973 is someone who can perform the main functions of the job:
    A. All of the time
    B. With reasonable accommodations
    C. Without any accommodations
    D. With considerable assistance and the necessary accommodations

16. Which organization attempts to reach an agreement between the employee and employer through persuasion and conciliation regarding the laws related to equal employment, civil rights, and discrimination?
    A. Occupational Safety and Health Administration (OSHA)
    B. The Alliance Program
    C. Equal Employment Opportunity Commission (EEOC)
    D. Safety and Health Achievement Recognition Program

17. A visiting family member steals $100 from a patient's purse. This is an example of a violation of which type of law?
    A. Civil law
    B. Criminal law
    C. Intentional tort
    D. Unintentional tort

18. A staff nurse sends a patient to have a minimally invasive surgical procedure without obtaining a signed informed consent document. Although the patient has verbally agreed to the procedure, the healthcare team could be liable for:
    A. Assault
    B. Battery
    C. False imprisonment
    D. All of the above

19. Which is a true statement concerning risk management (RM) and quality improvement (QI)?
    A. Both attempt to identify risk patterns and avoid adverse patient outcomes
    B. Both require cooperation from the patient
    C. Neither uses similar tools and techniques to identify and resolve problematic issues
    D. Neither require complete and clear documentation

20. How are risk management (RM) and quality improvement (QI) different?
    A. RM is concerned with care from a financial and legal perspective, minimizing the costs of liability, whereas QI is concerned with patient care issues and outcomes.
    B. QI investigates patient and visitor safety, environment, and exposures, whereas RM investigates patient-care-focused issues, such as optimal quality of care and adherence to professional standards.
    C. QI attempts to decrease adverse patient outcomes, whereas RM aims to increase quality patient outcomes.
    D. RM assists with the enhancement of care and associated quality outcomes, whereas QI focuses on loss prevention.

21. The patient in room 123 was ordered IV cephalexin, and the patient in room 124 was ordered IV doxycycline. A staff nurse got the two mixed up, and both patients received the wrong IV antibiotic. However, both of the infusions were stopped before any harm occurred. What level of risk management adverse patient outcome (APO) does this situation require?
    A. Level I
    B. Level II
    C. Level III
    D. Level IV

22. The process for identifying, investigating, reporting, and correcting APOs is called:
    A. Liability exposure
    B. Root cause analysis
    C. Incident reporting
    D. Core measuring

23. The incident report is a communication tool used to record:
    A. An error
    B. An accident
    C. The discovery of a hazardous condition
    D. All of the above

24. Which outcome measures have accurate examples?
    A. Clinical outcome measures = Length of stay, cost per day, and cost per case
    B. Utilization outcome measures = Morbidity rates, complication rates, and mortality rates
    C. Satisfaction outcome measures = Patient experience, state of well-being, and comfort
    D. Transitional planning outcome measures = Denial rate, appeals conversion rate, and surgical delays

25. Which of the following is a true statement concerning core measures?
    A. Core measures are set by the Center for Medicare & Medicaid Services (CMS).
    B. Core measures are state standardized performance measurements that are used to improve the quality of care.
    C. Core measures are related to intravenous infusions, wound care, and discharge planning.
    D. Core measures are often called regional quantity measures.

26. Which of the following is a core measure for a patient with pneumonia?
    A. Oxygenation assessment
    B. Pneumococcal vaccination
    C. Initial antibiotic within 4 hours of arrival
    D. All of the above

27. The CMSA Standards of Practice for Case Managers include which of the following elements:
    A. Duty, breach, cause, and harm
    B. Quality care, qualifications for case managers, collaboration with healthcare providers and patients, and legal and ethical considerations
    C. Core measures and case management outcome indicators
    D. Autonomy, beneficence, non-maleficence, justice, and veracity

28. Which CMSA Standard of Practice implies that the case manager should identify immediate, short-term, long-term, and ongoing needs and develop appropriate and necessary case management strategies and goals to address those needs?
    A. Standard A – Patient Selection
    B. Standard B – Patient Assessment
    C. Standard C – Problem/Opportunity Identification
    D. Standard D – Planning

29. Which of the following is an example of a core measure for pediatric asthma?
    A. Prophylactic antibiotic within 1 hour before
    B. Appropriate hair removal
    C. Appropriate thromboembolism prophylaxis
    D. None of the above

30. Which CSMA Standard of Practice indicates that the case manager should be aware of, and responsive to, cultural and demographic diversity of the population and specific client profiles?
    A. Standard K – Ethics
    B. Standard L – Advocacy
    C. Standard M – Cultural Competency
    D. Standard N – Resource Management and Stewardship

31. Which CSMA Standard of Practice specifies that the case manager should maximize the client's health, wellness, safety, adaptation, and self-care through quality case management, client satisfaction, and cost-efficiency?
    A. Standard E – Monitoring
    B. Standard F – Outcomes
    C. Standard G – Termination of Case Management Services
    D. Standard H – Facilitation, Coordination, and Collaboration

32. Variance outcome measures are:
    A. System-related
    B. Community-related
    C. Practitioner-related
    D. All of the above

33. The ethical code of the case management profession is called:
    A. Code of Ethics for Case Managers
    B. Code of Professional Conduct for Case Managers
    C. Code of Standards of Practice for Case Managers
    D. Code of Conduct for Nurses

34. The child labor provisions establish the basic minimum age for full-time, regular employment, which is:
    A. 14
    B. 15
    C. 16
    D. 18

Psychosocial Aspects (20%)

1. Which of the following is true concerning child abuse?
    A. Child abuse reporting is mandatory in some states.
    B. Child abuse involves only sexual abuse incidents.
    C. Healthcare providers who do not report child abuse can be criminally charged.
    D. Child abuse exists in all ethnic and socioeconomic groups.

2. Psychosocial evaluations of patients should involve an assessment of their:
    A. Value systems
    B. Traditions
    C. Beliefs
    D. All of the above
    E. None of the above

3. One of the risk factors for malnutrition is:
    A. Dentures
    B. Recent weight loss of three pounds
    C. Recent weight loss of five pounds
    D. Poverty

4. Which of the following patients would need a psychosocial evaluation?
    A. 44-year-old man with chronic heart disease
    B. Single 24-year-old woman
    C. 72-year-old woman who had an unintentional overdose
    D. 54-year-old man with limited financial resources

5. Bereavement is:
    A. Feeling of sadness
    B. Change in mood
    C. Public expression of grief
    D. Time period of mourning

6. A Jehovah's Witness patient is in the hospital. Which of the following should the nurse anticipate?
    A. He/she may refuse to eat certain meats.
    B. He/she may refuse intravenous antibiotics.
    C. He/she may refuse intravenous blood transfusions.
    D. He/she may refuse oral pain medications.

7. In some non-Western cultures, people believe that certain natural causes contribute to health problems. These include:
    A. Spirits, supernatural forces, and deities
    B. Heat, cold, dampness, and wind
    C. Earth, Moon, Sun, and the stars
    D. All of the above

8. Which of the following would constitute a severe and persistent mental illness (SPMI)?
    A. Feelings of sadness after the death of a loved one
    B. Narcissistic personality disorder (NPD)
    C. Anxiety
    D. Feelings of anxiety prior to a surgical procedure

9. With the Brokerage Model of behavioral health case management, the functions of the case manager include:
    A. Patient advocacy
    B. Transportation of consumers to and from treatment sites
    C. Symptom and medication monitoring
    D. Assessment and teaching regarding community living
    E. All of the above

10. What area of the Strengths Model involves prioritizing the patient's past and present accomplishments, resources, and future interests?
    A. Strengths assessment
    B. Personal planning
    C. Engagement
    D. Resources acquisition

11. Which model is most recognized and used by case managers and healthcare facilities because it controls psychiatric symptoms, reduces hospital use, increases housing stability, and improves quality of life?
    A. The Strengths Model
    B. The Brokerage Model
    C. The Assertive Community Treatment Model
    D. None of the above

12. Which assessment tool utilizes careful observation of non-verbal behavior to evaluate pain, where changes are noted in vocalization, respirations, body language, and consolability?
    A. The Pain Assessment in Advanced Dementia (PAINAD) scale
    B. The Mini-Cog Assessment
    C. The Pain Assessment Method
    D. The Mini-Mental Status Exam

13. The case manager asks the patient to draw the face of a clock with all 12 numbers and hands to show the time specified and to repeat the names of three common objects that were given early in the interview process. Which type of test is this?
    A. An assessment for dementia through cognitive testing
    B. An assessment for memory through diagnostic testing
    C. An assessment for pain through evaluation testing
    D. An assessment for intelligence through basic testing

14. Evaluation of a palliative care patient's religious or spiritual beliefs should include which of the following?
    A. Assessment of religious or spiritual beliefs only if the patient mentions this or specifically inquires
    B. Screening for religious or spiritual beliefs that could conflict with the palliative care nurse's own religious practices
    C. Encouragement for the patient to attend a religious service or community church if the patient specifies he/she does not belong to one
    D. Asking of the patient about spiritual rituals or customs around illness and death that are considered meaningful

15. A psychosocial situation that occurs when family members realize that they are unable to care for a patient in the home setting is called:
    A. The respite syndrome
    B. The brick wall syndrome
    C. The fatigue syndrome
    D. The caregiver syndrome

16. A sign that a patient has an alcohol use/abuse problem is:
    A. Obtaining a parking ticket
    B. Being late for work two days in a row
    C. Arrest for disorderly conduct
    D. Disagreement with spouse

17. Indicators of child health outcomes include:
    A. Income
    B. Parental health
    C. Employment
    D. Family support
    E. All of the above

18. A 28-year-old hospice patient with terminal cancer has expressed his preference to avoid intravenous hydration once he can no longer drink fluids by mouth. The hospice case manager should explain that:
    A. Without this form of hydration, he will likely have more pain during the dying process.
    B. Dehydration can contribute to increased respiratory sections during the dying process.
    C. Intravenous hydration must be provided because it is unethical to deprive a patient of basic needs.
    D. Intravenous hydration can be withheld per the patient's request.

19. A disagreement between family members concerning a patient's plan of care during the dying process when the patient lacks the capacity to make end-of-life decisions should be managed by:
    A. Asking each family member to consider what he/she would choose if he/she was in these circumstances
    B. Informing the family members that palliative care planning cannot succeed until the family reaches an agreement
    C. Pursuing legal action to facilitate the designation of a single family member as the medical decision-maker
    D. Encouraging the family to consider what the patient would want for himself/herself

20. When a child is sick, the case manager must establish the primary caregiver and assess:
    A. The caregiver's readiness to learn
    B. The caregiver's willingness to learn
    C. The caregiver's ability to learn
    D. All of the above

21. Which resource for the elderly can provide in-home visits by nurses for activities associated with health promotion?
    A. The American Association of Retired Persons (AARP)
    B. Local public health departments
    C. The Area Agency on Aging (AAA)
    D. The Salvation Army

22. A maternal-infant care case manager should coordinate patient education efforts, which include all of the following EXCEPT:
    A. Prenatal classes
    B. Lamaze classes
    C. Prenatal screenings
    D. Community transportation

23. All of the following are barriers to providing optimal palliative care to patients who live in poverty EXCPT:
    A. Lack of transportation
    B. Less stable support systems
    C. Fragile housing
    D. Less effective coping skills

24. One example of a situational crisis is:
    A. Unplanned illness
    B. Unplanned pregnancy
    C. Graduating from high school
    D. Graduating from college

25. What is the purpose of the CAGE assessment tool?
    A. Assess for dementia
    B. Assess for sex addiction
    C. Assess for alcohol abuse
    D. Assess for gambling addiction

26. Threatening to harm or injure someone and withhold clothes and food if the person is uncooperative is an example of:
    A. Neglect
    B. Financial abuse
    C. Physical abuse
    D. Psychological abuse

27. An alert and cognitively competent elderly home care patient complains that items have been disappearing from his home. He is most likely the victim of:
    A. Financial abuse
    B. Physical abuse
    C. Psychological abuse
    D. Elder abuse

28. A patient or parent's refusal for care can be overridden if:
    A. The patient is elderly
    B. The patient is a minor child
    C. The patient is mentally incompetent
    D. The physician orders the care

29. Jung's theory of personality development over the lifespan is called:
    A. Life Course
    B. Theory of Individualism
    C. Hierarchy of Needs
    D. Age Stratification

30. A 24-year-old single mother of two young children is being discharged following a surgical procedure. She expresses concern that she may be homeless because she cannot find a job. Which referral is most appropriate?
    A. Homeless shelter
    B. Social worker
    C. Mental health center
    D. Food assistance organization

31. The legal document that designates someone to make end-of-life care decisions for a patient who is mentally incompetent is a/an:
    A. Do-Not-Resuscitate (DNR) order
    B. Advanced directive
    C. General power of attorney
    D. Durable power of attorney

32. When assessing culture, the first step involves:
    A. Establishing trust
    B. Asking permission to do the cultural assessment
    C. Explaining the purpose of the cultural assessment
    D. Taking notes during the communication

33. What initiates palliative care for a patient?
    A. The patient requests palliative care.
    B. The patient's life expectancy is less than six months.
    C. The patient's life expectancy is less than one year.
    D. The patient is diagnosed with a life-threatening disease.

34. Elderly patients with chronic conditions that result in physical limitations and persistent pain should be evaluated for:
    A. Drug abuse
    B. Alcohol abuse
    C. Dementia
    D. Depression

35. Concerning a dual diagnosis, the initial treatment typically focuses on:
    A. Rehabilitation
    B. Detoxification
    C. Mental health treatment
    D. Medications

Healthcare Management and Delivery (20%)

1. The unit that most often requires the services of a case manager is the:
   A. Critical care unit
   B. Surgical unit
   C. Medical unit
   D. Sub-acute care facility

2. The case management plan in an ambulatory or outpatient facility is often used for:
   A. Home care visits
   B. Clinic visits
   C. Outpatient surgery visits
   D. All of the above
   E. None of the above

3. Criteria for patient selection on a surgical unit are based on all of the following EXCEPT:
   A. Patient need
   B. Intensity of service
   C. Severity of illness
   D. Case complexity

4. Which of the following is NOT a true statement regarding sub-acute care facilities?
   A. Sub-acute care is a level of care that blends short-term and acute care skills and philosophies.
   B. Most patients are admitted to sub-acute care facilities following a hospitalization.
   C. Three models of sub-acute care include short-term medically complex, short-term rehabilitative, and chronic.
   D. Sub-acute care often bridges acute and long-term care.

5. A holistic care model in which all components work toward the good of the patients of a particular population is the:
   A. Collaborative Care Model
   B. Disease Management Model
   C. Medical Home Model
   D. Chronic Care Model

6. In the disease management process, the evaluation of outcome measures step involves:
   A. Use of clinical and quality indicators to assess outcomes
   B. Use of cost indicators to assess financial outcomes
   C. Both A and B
   D. Neither A nor B

7. The disposition of the patient at discharge is called the:
    A. Discharge criteria
    B. Discharge title
    C. Discharge code
    D. Discharge status

8. What can the nurse case manager do to develop disease management plans?
    A. Use evidence-based practice guidelines to establish goals and objectives
    B. Use criteria to assess high-risk patients for select diseases
    C. Continue ongoing monitoring and assessment of the patient's condition
    D. Use clinical and quality indicators to evaluate outcomes

9. A concept that involves an integrated system of care to guide and track a patient over time through a comprehensive model that covers all levels of care is the:
    A. Healthcare delivery system
    B. Continuum of care
    C. Medical home
    D. Patient-Centered Primary Care Collaborative (PCPCC)

10. Which type of continuity is achieved when services are conducted in a timely and complementary manner?
    A. Information continuity
    B. Management continuity
    C. Relational continuity
    D. All of the above

11. What standards were developed for healthcare facilities by CMS to improve quality and to protect the safety and well-being of health plan members?
    A. Conditions of Participation (CoP)
    B. Standards of Practice
    C. Patient-Centered Primary Care Collaborative (PCPCC)
    D. None of the above

12. Which team has members that work in parallel to each other with little communication?
    A. Interdisciplinary team
    B. Trans-disciplinary team
    C. Multidisciplinary team
    D. All of the above

13. For the insurance company to cover rehabilitation services and treatment, the two fundamental requirements that must be met are:
    A. The care must be reasonable and necessary regarding duration, frequency, efficacy, and amount, and the care must be provided in an inpatient setting.
    B. The care must be reasonable and necessary regarding duration, frequency, efficacy, and amount, and the care must be provided in an outpatient setting.
    C. The care must be reasonable and necessary regarding quality, cost, and intensity, and the care must be provided in a skilled nursing facility.
    D. The care must be reasonable and necessary regarding quality, cost, and intensity, and the care must be provided in a home health setting.

14. What is a schematic model that supports the use of clinical decision pathways and is structured in a yes/no method?
    A. Critical pathway
    B. Algorithm
    C. Case management care plan
    D. All of the above

15. What organization developed the Medical Home Model in 2003, with the support from many professional organizations?
    A. American Nurses Association (ANA)
    B. Case Management Society of American (CMSA)
    C. National Committee for Quality Assurance (NCQA)
    D. Case Management Commission (CMC)

16. Which element of PCMH Recognition maintains that the practice works to facilitate self-management of care for patients with one of three clinically important conditions?
    A. Guidelines for important conditions
    B. Self-management support
    C. Test tracking and follow-up
    D. Referral tracking

17. Regarding the goals and principles of a palliative care program, the care and services are coordinated by a:
    A. Physician
    B. Staff nurse
    C. Legal representative
    D. Case manager

18. Examples of end-stage disease indicators related to heart disease are:
    A. Physical decline, weight loss, and multiple comorbidities
    B. Ejection fraction < 20%, arrhythmias resistant to treatment, and discomfort with physical activity
    C. PT > 5 seconds, ascites resistant to treatment, and hepatorenal syndrome
    D. Intractable fluid overload, oliguria < 40 cc/24 hours, and hyperkalemia

19. What are CORFs?
    A. Comprehensive Occupational Rehabilitation Factors
    B. Comprehensive Outpatient Rehabilitation Facilities
    C. Cooperative Outcomes Related to Facts
    D. Collaborative Outcomes Rehabilitation Facilities

20. A physician who specializes in rehabilitation and physical medicine is called a/an:
    A. Orthopedic surgeon
    B. Neurosurgeon
    C. Physiatrist
    D. Internist

21. A process of assessing a patient's needs after discharge from a healthcare facility and putting the necessary services in place before discharge is called:
    A. Transitional planning
    B. Discharge planning
    C. Outcomes planning
    D. Resource planning

22. Which of the following is NOT a component of a critical pathway?
    A. Timeline
    B. Identified care categories and activities
    C. Allowance for deviations and variances
    D. Identification of individuals at risk for potential adverse outcomes

23. Which of the following discharge codes would indicate that the patient qualifies for skilled care?
    A. Code 01-Discharged to home (routine discharge)
    B. Code 02-Discharged to a short-term healthcare facility
    C. Code 03-Discharged to SNR with Medicare certification
    D. Code 04-Discharged to an intermediate care facility (ICF)

24. Tools created to show current practice parameters and/or recommended "best practices" and to target lengths of stay and anticipated levels of care are:
    A. Algorithms
    B. Critical pathways
    C. Case management care plans
    D. Discharge codes

25. What model identifies several essential elements of a healthcare system that promotes high-quality chronic disease management and care?
    A. The Medical Home Model
    B. The Preventive Care Model
    C. The Brokerage Model
    D. The Chronic Care Model

26. The patient is being discharged from an acute care health facility with an infusion pump for numerous intravenous medications. Where can the case manager transfer this patient?
    A. Intermediate care facility
    B. Sub-acute and rehabilitation facilities
    C. Skilled nursing facility
    D. Long-term group homes and skilled nursing facilities

27. The Milliman Care Guidelines are considered:
    A. Ambulatory care guidelines
    B. Chronic care guidelines
    C. General recovery guidelines
    D. Inpatient and surgical care guidelines

28. Transitions of care typically require:
    A. Handoff
    B. Physician change
    C. Vehicle transportation
    D. Facility transfer

29. The most important aspect when reintegrating a spinal cord-injured patient back into the community after a long stay in a rehabilitation center is:
    A. Follow-up and continued services
    B. Family support
    C. Patient compliance
    · D. Comprehensive plan of care ·

30. The primary purpose of the interdisciplinary team is:
    A. Cost-saving
    B. Time-saving
    C. Sharing ideas to solve problems
    D. Improving patient satisfaction

31. The best placement for a 42-year-old female with an IQ of 70 who cannot live alone would be a/an:
    A. Skilled nursing facility
    B. Acute care facility
    C. Group home
    D. Assisted living facility

32. For continued care after a patient is discharged from an acute care facility, the most important relationship for a case manager to develop is with:
    A. Physician office staff
    B. Skilled nursing facilities and home health agencies
    C. HMO healthcare providers
    D. Hospital administrators

33. With which type of team do members operate at the opposite end of the continuum and do professional functions tend to overlap?
    A. Interdisciplinary team
    B. Multidisciplinary team
    C. Trans-disciplinary team
    D. None of the above

34. Which model of healthcare involves numerous providers who serve along the continuum?
    A. The Component Management Model
    B. The Medical Home Model
    C. The Chronic Care Model
    D. The Strengths Model

35. The rehabilitative patients who have potential for improvement, but still have significant nursing needs and are unable to tolerate intense rehabilitation are:
    A. Short-term rehabilitation patients
    B. Chronic care patients
    C. Short-term medically complex patients
    D. Chronic medically complex patients

Healthcare Reimbursement (15%)

1. What reimbursement method is used to reimburse the cost of providing outpatient procedures or visits and does not cover the physician cost elements?
    A. Ambulatory patient classification (APC)
    B. Ambulatory patient groups (APGs)
    C. Diagnostic-related groups (DRGs)
    D. Prospective payment system (PPS)

2. What is used to differentiate nursing home patients by their levels of resource use in skilled nursing facilities?
    A. Outcome and Assessment Information Set (OASIS)
    B. Resource Utilization Groups (RUGs)
    C. Minimum Data Set (MDS)
    D. Prospective Payment System (PPS)

3. Which type of savings is facilitated by changes in level of care and length of stay?
    A. Soft savings
    B. Hard savings
    C. Cost savings
    D. None of the above

4. Which process involves strategies to eliminate or cut down on services that are not vital for financial viability of the healthcare facility?
    A. Cost-benefit analysis (CBA)
    B. Hard savings
    C. Soft savings
    D. Reduction in force (RIF)

5. All of the following clinical variables affect length of stay EXCEPT:

    A. Mortality
    B. Poor health status of the patient
    C. Discharge planning
    D. Comorbidity and complications

6. Which method is an economic process used to evaluate outcomes and costs of treatments, interventions, and delivery systems?
    A. Case management analysis
    B. Cost-effectiveness analysis
    C. Cost-benefit analysis
    D. Case benefit analysis

7. The case management quality index (CMQI) score is calculated:
    A. By dividing the total costs per environment accrued in a specific time period by the total number of patients cared for in that environment during that same time period
    B. Based on the unit of analysis identified in the CEA study
    C. By a measure of case management value
    D. All of the above

8. Utilization reviews, equipment, and communication methods are all examples of:
    A. Cost of case managers
    B. Cost of equipment
    C. Cost of supplies
    D. Cost of services

9. A percentage of charges for services for which a member of the health plan must pay is called:
   A. Capitation
   B. Co-insurance
   C. Co-pay
   D. Deductible

10. Which type of utilization management service occurs before services are rendered, and in which does the reviewer decide if or not the admission is medically necessary?
    A. Prospective review
    B. Concurrent review
    C. Retrospective review
    D. Ongoing review

11. Which type of review is performed within 24 hours of admission?
    A. Prospective review
    B. Concurrent review
    C. Continued stay review
    D. Retrospective review

12. The maximum per calendar year for which a health plan member pays is (Hint: Co-payments, co-insurance, and deductibles all go toward this maximum.):
    A. In-pocket maximum
    B. Out-of-pocket maximum
    C. Insurance maximum
    D. Capitated maximum

13. Fee for service, case rate, capitated rate, discounted, and per diem are all examples of:
    A. Limits
    B. Reimbursement mechanisms
    C. Risk sharing
    D. Credentialing

14. The process where an HMO and healthcare provider both accept a portion of the responsibility for financial risk and reward is called:
    A. Managed care sharing
    B. Risk sharing
    C. Cost sharing
    D. Liability sharing

15. Medical admissions on _____ have the lowest average length of stay.
   A. Sunday
   B. Monday
   C. Thursday
   D. Friday

16. Which of the following is associated with a longer length of stay?
   A. Case management
   B. Interdepartmental coordination and integration of patient services
   C. Increased use of laboratory and radiology services
   D. All of the above

17. Which system reimburses for home care services based on a nursing assessment completed on the first home visit?
   A. Case mix groups (CMGs)
   B. Resource utilization groups (RUGs)
   C. Home health resource groups (HHRGs)
   D. Ambulatory patient classification (APC)

18. Which managed care structure contains features of both PPOs and HMOs, and in which the physician is reimbursed through a fixed per member per month payment or other reimbursement method?
   A. Exclusive Provider Organization (EPO)
   B. Independent Practice Associations (IPAs)
   C. Point of Service (POS) plans
   D. Direct Contract Model

19. With the _____, the physicians are employed by the HMO to provide all services to health plan members.
   A. Staff Model HMO
   B. Group Practice Model HMO
   C. Network Model HMO
   D. Independent Practice Association HMO

20. With the _____ reimbursement method, organizations are paid a specific amount per day regardless of actual costs, and this is based on the number of days of service and averaging costs.
   A. Discounted fee for service
   B. Per diem
   C. Fee for service
   D. Percent of charges

21. DRG case rate is:
    A. Services that are excluded from the provider contract that can be provided through arrangement with other providers
    B. The rate of reimbursement that covers a certain category of services
    C. A predetermined payment structure that is all-inclusive and is used for a specific set of related services
    D. None of the above

22. With the utilization management review process, who usually determines covered benefits?
    A. Physician
    B. Patient
    C. Case manager
    D. Customer service representative

23. All of the following are goals of a utilization management program EXCEPT:
    A. To determine medical necessity and need for services
    B. To promote quality care and effective outcomes
    C. To locate cooperation of care options for members and providers
    D. To identify diseases that contribute to high healthcare expenses

24. The purpose of stop-loss insurance is to:
    A. Protect the insurance company against high utilization
    B. Replace a part of insurance coverage
    C. Limit the type of services covered
    D. Defer medical expenses until funds are available

25. The Medicare benefit period ends _____ days after discharge from an inpatient facility.
    A. 150
    B. 100
    C. 60
    D. 30

26. The DRG is scored based on:
    A. Its potential consumption and intensity of resources
    B. Its potential consumption and severity of illness
    C. The age and sex of the patient
    D. The primary and secondary diagnosis

27. How many hours does an insurance company have to decide on an appeal following denial of urgent care services?
    A. 12
    B. 24
    C. 48
    D. 72

Rehabilitation (5%)

1. Which area of rehabilitation treatment involves teaching, restoring, and assisting with work-related skills?
   A. Self-care skills
   B. Mobility skills
   C. Socialization skills
   D. Vocational skills

2. Which rehabilitation setting is a highly specialized outpatient facility that provides outpatient and restorative rehabilitation services?
   A. Intermediate rehabilitation facility (IRF)
   B. Comprehensive Outpatient Rehabilitation Facility (CORF)
   C. Skilled Nursing Facility (SNF)
   D. Long-Term Care (LTC) Facility

3. In most skilled nursing facilities, _____% of the charges is for rehabilitation care services.
   A. 20
   B. 30
   C. 40
   D. 50

4. Medicare assists with payment for medically necessary outpatient occupational therapy (OT), physical therapy (PT), and speech therapy (ST) services if:
   A. The patient requests the service
   B. The case manager arranges the service
   C. The physician periodically reviews the plan of care for patient progression
   D. The case manager periodically reviews the plan of care for patient progression

5. An interdisciplinary, job-specific concept that involves activity with the goal of return-to-work and that provides a transition between acute care and successful return-to-work is:
   A. Work hardening
   B. Work transition
   C. Work adjustment
   D. Workers' compensation

6. Which of the following is NOT a true statement concerning workforce management?
   A. Workforce management involves work adjustment, work transition, and work hardening.
   B. Workforce management includes benefit plan design, demographics of the employer's worker populations, and health and productivity programs.
   C. The concept of workforce management involves only occupational lost-time cases and effective return-to-work status.
   D. The concept of workforce management involves all aspects of occupational disability, non-occupational disability, and proactive health and safety information and training.

7. Workers' compensation is enforced by:
   A. Federal statute
   B. State statute
   C. Regional statute
   D. Place of employment

8. What act offers protection to workers, their families, and their communities by mandating employers to give notice 60 days in advance of plant closing and mass layoffs?
   A. The Workers' Compensation Act
   B. The Worker Transition Act
   C. The Worker Adjustment and Retraining Notification Act
   D. The Workers' Union Act

9. A covered employer must give notice if an employment site will be shut down and will result in an employment loss for _____ or more employees during a 30-day period.
   A. 20
   B. 30
   C. 50
   D. 100

10. Which of the following persons would qualify for a work hardening program?
   A. 64-year-old man who's physical recovery is sufficient to permit progressive reactivation and participation in the program for a minimum of four hours a day for three to five days a week.
   B. 68-year-old man who's physical recovery is sufficient to permit progressive reactivation and participation in the program for a minimum of four hours a day for three to five days a week.
   C. 44-year-old man with no defined return-to-work goal and who's physical recovery is sufficient to permit progressive reactivation and participation in the program for a maximum of three hours a day for two days a week.
   D. Both A and B
   E. None of the above

11. Which organization encourages and assists with the employment and retention of workers with disabilities by providing information regarding job accommodations to employers, employment providers, people with disabilities, and other interested parties?
    A. Job Accommodation Network (JAN)
    B. Occupational Safety and Health Administration (OSHA)
    C. U.S. Department of Health and Human Services
    D. U.S. Department of Labor

12. What is used to evaluate patients with early-stage disease, to assess the level of the disease, and to determine the patient's ability to perform self-care tasks?
    A. Functional capacity evaluation (FCE)
    B. Instrumental Activities of Daily Living (IADL) tool
    C. Barthel Index of Activities of Daily Living tool
    D. CAGE questionnaire

13. Which of the following is NOT one of the practice domains for disability management specialists?
    A. Disability case management
    B. Disability prevention and workplace intervention
    C. Program development, management, and evaluation
    D. Cost savings creation for displaced workers

14. How much will a patient with Medicare Parts A and B typically have to pay for durable medical equipment if it is approved by the insurance company and ordered by the physician?
    A. 100%
    B. 80%
    C. 60%
    D. 20%

15. All of the following are considered durable medical equipment EXCEPT:
    A. Crutches
    B. Electric hospital beds
    C. Electronic hearing aids
    D. Wound care supplies

16. An 82-year-old frail woman is being discharged with a walker, shower chair, and hospital bed. The caregiver/daughter insists that someone must show them how to use this equipment. What should the case manager do?
    A. Have the DME delivered prior to discharge
    B. Arrange for the DME company staff to instruct on the use of the equipment
    C. Send the DME early and bill the patient on the day it is sent
    D. Both A and B
    E. A, B, and C

17. What is the applied science of equipment design, which is intended to increase productivity by reducing operator discomfort and fatigue?
    A. Economics
    B. Ergonomics
    C. Biomedical modeling
    D. Human assistance

18. The term "assistive technology service" means:
    A. Any service that directly assists an individual with a disability in the selection, acquisition, or use of an assistive technology device
    B. The applied science of equipment design, which is intended to increase productivity by reducing operator discomfort and fatigue
    C. Any item, piece of equipment, or product system, whether acquired commercially off the shelf, modified, or customized, that is used to increase, maintain, or improve functional capabilities of individuals with disabilities
    D. Any service where the case manager assists with obtaining durable medical equipment

19. Which type of case manager works in collaboration with other healthcare providers to coordinate the healthcare services for a patient from the illness or injury onset to the end of case management services and serves as a gatekeeper for rehabilitation, health services, and case management issues?
    A. Occupational health case manger
    B. Acute care case manger
    C. Critical care case manager
    D. Skilled nursing case manager

20. Which type of case management is a process that involves performing individual case analysis and benefits assessment, reviewing disability case management intervention protocols, collaborating with stakeholders, performing job analyses, developing return-to-work plans, implementing interventions, coordinating benefits and services, monitoring progress, and managing a caseload of clients?
    A. Acute care case management
    B. Critical care case management
    C. Home health case management
    D. Disability case management

Test Your Knowledge—Answers

Case Management Concepts (25%)

1. **B.**

   Many people often confuse the terms *managed care* and *case management*. In general, managed care is systems-oriented, focusing on health insurance plans and the management of various benefits. Case management is people-oriented and focused on disbursement of managed care systems in a manner that benefits everyone, especially the patient Care management is a term used to describe case management for the elderly, chronic, and long-term care patient populations. Care coordination is an aspect of the case management process (Lowery, 2008; Powell & Tahan, 2010).

2. **D.**

   The five principles that serve a basis of case management practice are: focus on patient and family; negotiating, procuring, and coordinating services and resources; use of the clinical reasoning process; development of various relationships; and episode- or continuum-based (not insurance-based) (Cohen, 1996).

3. **E.**

   With case management, patient selection criteria are determined by the employer of the healthcare facility. Populations are targeted for various conditions and reasons, such as the diagnostic categories acute injury or illness, chronic injury or illness, multiple diagnoses, and end stage disease processes (Lowery, 2008).

4. **A.**

   According to Lowery (2008), patients who are candidates for case management services include those who have a potential need for high utilization of resources, the frail and elderly, or those with a complicated procedure scheduled, frequent and/or prolonged hospitalizations and emergency department visits, complicated psychological conditions, vocational support needs, functional impairments, and disability.

5. **D.**

   These roles and functions of the case manager vary according to the setting in which the nurse works, the patient population being served, and the case management program and processes. They also differ based on case mix of patients. Geriatric patients have different needs than pediatric patients, just as cancer patients have different needs than acutely ill patients (Powell & Tahan, 2010).

6. **B.**

   Case finding and intake involves identification of patient who would benefit, obtainment of informed consent for services, communication of patient's needs to others, and identification of patients who need alternate levels of care. Facilitation and coordination of care activities (choice A) and review and modification of healthcare services (choice C) fall under the provision of services domain. Data collecting, analyzing, and reporting (choice D) falls under the evaluation and case closure domain (Powell & Tahan, 2010).

7. **C.**
The utilization management domain of case management involves: evaluation of appropriate level of care; communication with payers and other healthcare providers; allocation of resources based on patient needs (not insurance requests); management of reimbursement appeals and denials; review of patient condition for appropriateness of hospitalization; and identification of cases that are high risk for complications (Powell & Tahan, 2010).

8. **B.**
The evaluation and case closure domain of case management involves data collecting, analyzing, and reporting, quality of case management services evaluation, access to timely and necessary services application of evidence-based practice guidelines in plan, closing the case manager-patient relationship, reporting termination of services to stakeholders, and educating patient regarding illness prevention. Serving as patient and family advocate (choice A) falls under the provision of services domain. Management of reimbursement appeals and denials (choice C) falls under the utilization management domain. Assessment of patient's support network (choice D) falls under the psychosocial and economic issues domain (Powell & Tahan, 2010).

9. **C.**
Review of patient condition for appropriateness of hospitalization would fall under the utilization management domain of case management. The vocational issues domain components include: identification of need for changes in the home environment; elimination of access barriers; determination of need for specialized services; arrangement for vocational assessment and services; coordination of job analysis to implement modifications; and management of return-to-work activities (Powell & Tahan, 2010).

10. **B.**
There are several reasons why healthcare workers use case management. The purposes include: to maximize (not minimize-choice A) efficiency of valuable and available resource usage; to promote informed decision-making by the patient and others by interjecting objectivity and information (the correct choice); to work with the patient (not insurance company-choice C), as well as the family, physician, and other healthcare providers to implement a plan of care than meets the patient's needs; to make the healthcare delivery system more effective (not costly-choice D); to assist the patient in meeting planned outcomes through appropriate interventions and with a process that is measurable; to promote safe, cost-effective, accessible, and quality care; and to assist patients and families in

arranging and managing the complex resources require to maintain independent functioning and adequate health (Lowery, 2008).

11. **B.**

Primary nurse case management model is where services and caseloads of the nurse case manager are designated for specific patient case mixes or types. The nurse is the primary caregiver for these patients, coordinating the care throughout hospitalization, regardless of the patient's physical location. The leveled practice model focuses on the management and coordination of patient care needs. The nurse case manager is responsible for monitoring the patient care of several assigned patients (the caseload) through collaboration with the patient, family, staff, and interdisciplinary team. With the emergency department case management model, case managers provide gatekeeping oversight to this area of the hospital. The case manager interacts with physicians, nurses, admitting office staff, payer-based case managers, and social workers to ensure medically necessary care that is cost effective (Powell & Tahan, 2010; Woodall, 2005).

12. **D.**

A case manager should react and respond only to facts instead of feelings to avoid confrontations and biased decision-making. Professional communication skills that facilitate team communication include active listening, asking questions to clarify rather than challenge someone's ideas, respecting others' opinions, and not interpreting others' statements or interrupting others to give unsolicited advice.

13. **B.**

The five ways to manage patients with the acute care case management model include: unit-based: case manager manages patients while on a specific unit; complete-based: case manager follows patients from admission to discharge; disease-based: case manager following patients according to illness; practice-based: case manager follows patients according to the physician; and primary-based: case manager is the primary nurse for certain patients (Powell & Tahan, 2010).

14. **C.**

With the skilled nursing facility case management model, the nurse case manager acts as a liaison between the acute care and sub-acute care levels, and nurses who work in this environment assist the patient during the convalescent period by assessing the patient's condition and determining appropriate services. The rehabilitation case management model embraces the concept of the case manager-social worker team, and case managers in this environment work to bring the patient back to a functional level that is close to the person's baseline level. The community-based case management model is based on the concept of helping patients and families access appropriate services for independent functioning, and it works to prevent exacerbations of conditions through early assessment of the condition and necessary interventions. With independent case management, the nurse works with firms that are not a formal part of an insurance company or other health-related facility (Cohen, 2005; Powell & Tahan, 2010).

15. **E.**

Also called the public health case management model, the Community-Based Case Management Model is based on the concept of helping patients and families access appropriate services for independent functioning. Certain populations that need case managers include homeless families, substance abuse patients, mental health patients, and geriatric patients (Powell & Tahan, 2010).

16. **B.**

Benefits of private and independent case management model include increased flexibility and autonomy in decision-making, coordination of services, independent planning, greater income, and professional satisfaction (Cohen, 2005).

17. **C.**

Hospital payment is calculated by multiplying the relative weight with the facility's base rate. Each healthcare facility is assigned a base rate for reimbursement by CMS, and this rate is determined by population served, geographic location, cost of living in the area, type of hospital (teaching, academic, or community), and types of services (Cesta, 2005).

18. **E.**

The case mix index (CMI) is the sum of all DRG-related weights divided by the number of patients cared for during a specified period of time, typically one calendar year. With a high CMI the case mix complexity of the hospital is also greater. Case mix values depend on severity of illness, need for intervention, treatment difficulty, and presence of complications and/or comorbidities (Cesta, 2005).

19. **C.**

DRGs are separated into major diagnostic categories (MDCs). The number of DRGs in each MDC ranges from 1 to 20 or more. MDCs are grouped according to anatomical and pathophysiological sections and how patients should be clinically managed. Also, MDCs are categorized as either medical or surgical (Cesta, 2005).

20. **C.**

Case management outcomes are elements of the caseload matrix. The caseload matrix is used in caseload calculations to identify variables in various settings that affect caseloads. MDCs are categories. The case mix index (CMI) is the sum of all DRG-related weights divided by the number of patients cared for during a specified period of time, typically one calendar year (Cesta, 2005).

21. **D.**

Severity of illness and prognosis dictate the complexity and types of services provided, and the case mix influences hospital costs. Basically, the number of patients does not affect hospital costs as much as the types of patients and the use of resources (Cesta, 2005).

22. **B.**

Acute/sudden onset occurs within 24 hours, recent onset occurs within one week, new onset occurs greater than one week, and newly discovered is where new findings are found during this illness episode (Powell & Tahan, 2010).

23. **A.**

Patient acuity is a concept that is significant to patient safety, and as acuity rises, more nurses are needed to provide adequate, safe care. Severity of illness indicates how sick the patient is, what level care is appropriate, and what treatments and services are necessary. Intensity of service indicates what is being done for the patient, what level of care is given, and what resources the patient needs. Discharge screens are parameters that are objective, functional, and indicate readiness and stability for discharge or transfer to another care level (Jennings, 2013; Powell & Tahan, 2010).

24. **C.**

Examples of severity of illness criteria include an oral temperature 104 degrees Fahrenheit, sustained pulse greater than 100 bpm, respiratory rate greater than 26 with pulse oximeter less than 85% on room air, systolic blood pressure greater than 250 or less than 80 mmHg, and diastolic blood pressure greater than 120 or less than 40 mmHg.

25. **D.**

Discharge screens are parameters that are objective, functional, and indicate readiness and stability for discharge or transfer to another care level. These screens indicate if the patient is clinically ready for discharge or transfer and if the patient is stable enough for this process (Powell & Tahan, 2010).

26. **B.**

InterQual's review process of IS criteria involve four types of review: preadmission, admission, subsequent and discharge reviews. Preadmission review is initiated before patient admission to the healthcare facility. The admission review is usually the initial chart review, done within 24 hours of admission. Subsequent reviews are done throughout the hospitalization, typically every three days. The discharge review is initiated when the patient is ready for discharge or transfer (Powell & Tahan, 2010).

27. **C.**

InterQual's review process of IS criteria involve four types of review: preadmission, admission, subsequent and discharge reviews (Powell & Tahan, 2010).

28. **B.**

Conflict can be within oneself (intrapersonal), between the self and another person (interpersonal), among members of a particular group (intragroup), or among members of two more groups (intergroup). Competitive conflict occurs when the desired outcome is to overcome one's opponent (Rundio & Wilson, 2010).

29. **A.**

Strategies for conflict resolution include: focusing on goals rather than on personalities through careful consideration of the objectives that led to the conflict, meeting the needs of both parties equally (if possible), building consensus, engaging in dialogues that address conflict in order to create a healthy work environment, coaching and educating healthcare providers and nurses through role-playing exercises, staff meetings, educational videos, and effective communication, and identifying potential conflicts by developing procedures and processes for identification of potential common conflicts (Johnasen, 2012; Rundio & Wilson, 2010).

30. **B.**

Nurse case managers often try to prevent ethical conflict when this arises. Preventing and resolving ethical conflict facilitates early recognition of problematic situations and circumstances, as well as timely communication among those associated with the decision-making process. Successful mediation of ethical conflicts requires sensitivity to the problem and the ability to communicate factors that contribute to the conflict (Taylor, 2005).

31. **A.**

Collaboration is a process that involves joint decision-making among numerous parties where these persons have collective responsibility for outcomes. Collaborative case management models bring positive outcomes, such as reduced cost with improved quality of care and increased patient and staff satisfaction. With this model, all members of the team are held accountable for various aspects of case management. Physicians and nurses identify patients who are high-risk for resource utilization (Koenig, 2005).

32. **B.**

The Medical-Social Case Management Model focuses on the long-term care patient who is at risk for hospitalization. The model involves resource utilization of services that are not usually covered by health insurance but are necessary to maintain the patient in the home setting. The case manager oversees the care planning, assessment, coordination, and care monitoring processes. The case management facilitates arrangements with direct healthcare service delivery (Cohen & Celesta, 2005).

33. **C.**

The disease management model is often used in clinical practices, such as identifying patients with diabetes to attend education classes or distributing materials to women who need Pap smears. Additionally, disease management programs must be in sync with the needs of the healthcare facility. This involves the use of a planning framework and understanding the program goals (Lind, 2005).

34. **C.**

    According to Powell & Tahan (2010), the proper sequence of the stages of the case management process include: (1) case selection, (2) problem identification, (3) case plan development and coordination, (4) case plan implementation, (5) case plan evaluation, (6) case plan reassessment and reevaluation, and (7) case closure.

35. **B.**

    Certain behavioral, mental health, and substance abuse conditions may warrant a case management assessment. Red-flag psychosocial indicators include unintentional overdose, intentional overdose, alcohol and drug abuse, eating disorders, chronic mental illness, Alzheimer's disease and dementia, noncompliance, uncooperative, aggressive, or manipulative behaviors, Munchhausen syndrome, and Munchhausen syndrome by proxy (Powell & Tahan, 2010).

36. **C.**

    According to Powell & Tahan (2010), some socioeconomic factors alert the case manager to a need for case management, such as homelessness, child/elder abuse or neglect, out-of-area residence, and rural residence.

37. **B.**

    There are five categories of healthcare data described by Stead (1991). These are: historical data, which concerns a particular patient, device, or thing; encounter patient data; subgroup data, which is related to a specified set of events or patient population; work-flow management data; and knowledge databases, which are used in decision-making.

38. **C.**

    Outcome measures in case management should demonstrate two key points: (1) the case manager has four key functions, and (2) effective performance of these four functions positively impacts outcomes (Aliotta, 2005).

39. **B.**

    There are two database types. The data warehouse is used by nurse managers and analyst for population-based management and contains financial and clinical data. The data in this database is trended, comparative, and aggregate. The data repository is designed to facilitate the healthcare provider's decision-making regarding each patient. The focus of this database is on clinical and operational data that are available in real-time. Validity and reliability are two concepts used to measure data quality (Batron & Skiba, 2005).

40. **B.**

A successful case manager can synthesize and articulate information without the need for constant clarifications and explanations. Common difficulties of verbal communication include hearing impairment, language barriers, and developmental, cognitive, and/or psychological impairment (Alabama Department of Public Health, 2013).

41. **A.**

Gender represents nominal level of measurement, which is numerical naming where numbers do not represent a degree or quantity. The data type is nonparametric and other examples are ethnicity and religion. With ordinal level of measurement, the numbers are rank-ordered, as with patient acuity. This is also nonparametric data. Interval level of measurement is where equal differences between numbers represent differences in the variables, such as with length of stay. This data type is parametric. Ratio level of measurement is where numbers represent equal amounts to form an absolute zero, as with the Fahrenheit scale. This is also parametric data (Cleveland, 1985).

42. **C.**

Documentation of comorbidities and complications is important for reimbursement. For many patients, DRG relative weight is doubled with the addition of a comorbidity/complication (CC) designation. Comorbidity is a preexisting condition that causes the length of stay to prolong at least by one day in 75% of cases. A complication is a condition that occurs during the hospital stay that increases the length of stay by at least one day in 75% of cases. Mortality is a measure of the number of deaths in a given population (Cesta, 2005).

43. **D.**

One single overall QOL score may not reflect the differences in these categories. Also, one category can reflect decreased outcomes, where another can show improved outcomes. The categories are: physical functioning, which involves limitations related to physical disabilities or issues; social functioning, which involves limitations related to lack of social interaction; psychological functioning, which involves limitations related to emotional problems; economic resources, which involves access to care and healthcare costs; and general well-being, which involves general health perceptions (Nold, 2005).

44. **D.**

Typical risk management activities include falls assessment programs, injury reduction programs, pressure ulcer prevention programs, infection control surveillance, failure mode analysis, prevention of deep vein thrombosis, and daily review of patient flow activities. Quality improvement (QI) is a means of improving various aspects of quality care, such as policies and procedures, job descriptions, credentialing of professional staff, performance evaluations, educational programs, and continual monitoring activities. Performance improvement (PI) involves the four-step process of design, improvement, measurement, and control. Quality assurance is an initiative regarding the appropriate action to minimize the inevitable consequences (Powell & Tahan, 2010).

45. **D.**

When communicating with a patient, both non-verbal and verbal responses give the case manager useful information and can be of equal importance. When someone is not telling the truth or does not want to answer a question, he or she may look away, become tense, and remain silent. Therefore, information obtained during an interview should not include only the patient's factual responses but concerns, attitudes, and non-verbal responses, as well (Powell & Tahan, 2010).

Principles of Practice (15%)

1. **D.**

Accreditation also is a measure of quality of the program to purchasers of the program and the public. The organizations that offer accreditation programs for case management programs include Commission on Accreditation of Rehabilitation Facilities (CARF), Utilization Review Accreditation Commission (URAC), Accreditation Commission for Health Care (ACHC), National Committee for Quality Assurance (NCQA), and Joint Commission on Accreditation of Healthcare Organizations (JCAHO). The CARF standards are aimed toward medical rehabilitation case management, and the URAC standards apply more to payer-based programs (Boling & Severson, 2005).

2. **D.**

Accreditation is the cumulative review of the case management program structure and processes that are in place. This process reviews the documentation of policies and procedures and assesses how well the healthcare facility implements these policies and procedures. The accreditation process encompasses a review of documentation in order to assess policies, procedures, and process of the healthcare facility (Boling & Severson, 2005).

3. **D.**

Justice is where the patient received what he or she is owed and involves fair treatment. An example of this is when the case manager believes the patient is noncompliant and cannot advocate for him or her. Autonomy represents individual liberty, self-determination, personal inviolability, and anti-paternalism, and an example is when the patient has the right to refuse case management services. Non-maleficence is fundamental to healthcare ethics where the professional is obligated to "do no harm," and an example of harming the patient would be when the case manager writes reports that bias the payer against the patient. Beneficence obligates the professional to do as much good as he or she can, and an example of this is a choice of return to work versus unemployment benefits (Banja, 2008).

4. **A.**

   Organizational ethical conflicts are related to individuals of the healthcare facility and pertain to an organization's behaviors. Examples include denial of services, conflicts of interest, and allocation of resources. Clinical ethical conflicts are related to the medical treatment, such as end of life matters, lack of patient/family understanding of medical treatment, and conflicts regarding best treatment options (Banja, 2008).

5. **C.**

   The Code of Professional Conduct for Case Managers requires case managers to six standards of professional conduct. These are *advocacy*, which focuses on the role of the case manager as a patient advocate, *professional responsibility,* which involves the areas of practice, competence, representation of qualifications, use of CCM designation, conflict of interest, legal and benefit system requirements, and compliance proceedings, *case manager and patient relationship*, which focuses on description of services to patients, the relationships with patients, termination of services or case closure, and objectivity, *confidentiality, privacy, and record-keeping*, which describes the role of the case manager in legal compliance, client identity, electronic recordings, disclosure, storage, disposal, and reporting, *professional relationships*, which addresses dual relationships, testimony, unprofessional behaviors, solicitation, advertising, and fees, and *research*, which focuses on subject privacy and legal compliance issues (Powell & Tahan, 2010).

6. **B.**

   The Employee Retirement Income Security Act (ERISA) of 1974 involves the regulation of pension plans. ERISA was enacted so that employers who hire employees in multistate locations are not bothered with multiple state laws. The Federal Workforce Flexibility Act of 2004 added many strategies that support human capital management. The social health maintenance organization (SHMO) is a national managed care demonstration program that provides and finances long-term care for the elderly. The Family and Medical Leave Act (FMLA) entitles eligible employees of certain covered employers to take unpaid, job-protected leave for specified medical and family reasons with continuation of group health insurance coverage (Cohen & Cesta, 2005; Muller, 2010; U.S. Department of Labor, 2013; U.S. Office of Personnel Management, 2013).

7. **D.**

   According to the U.S. Department of Labor (2013), the FMLA applies to: private-sector employer with 50 or more employees in 20 or more work weeks in the current or preceding calendar year, including a successor or joint employer in interest to a covered employer; public agency, including local, state, or federal agencies, regardless of the number of employees; and public or private elementary or secondary schools, regardless of the number of employees.

8. **D.**

In 1993, the Health Security Act was initiated. This reform package was created by a task force for the purpose of developing a comprehensive plan to provide universal healthcare for all Americans. In 1994, Congress ended two prospects for the legislation. Comprehensive healthcare reform in the U.S. was not enacted by Congress until the Patient Protection and Affordable Care Act in 2010 (Cohen & Cesta, 2005).

9. **B.**

In 1990, the Americans with Disabilities Act (ADA) was signed into law. The term disability has three distinct definitions: physical or mental impairment that substantially limits one or more major life activities, a record of such impairment, and being regarded as having such an impairment (U.S. Department of Justice, 2013). The Family and Medical Leave Act (FMLA) entitles eligible employees of certain covered employers to take unpaid, job-protected leave for specified medical and family reasons with continuation of group health insurance coverage (U.S. Department of Labor, 2013). The Equal Pay Act (EPA) requires that men and women performing equal work receive equal pay. This act prohibits discrimination based on gender regarding compensation for work services (Rundio & Wilson, 2010). The Rehabilitation Act of 1973 ensures that qualified individuals with handicaps are not excluded from participation in various programs and activities or denied benefits from the employer (U.S. Equal Opportunity Commission, 2013b).

10. **D.**

According to the Equal Employment Opportunity Commission, reasonable accommodation means modifications to all of the choices listed (U.S. Equal Employment Opportunity Commission, 2013a).

11. **A.**

The Health Insurance Portability & Accountability Act (HIPAA) of 1996 provides healthcare coverage continuity, simplifies administrative functions within the healthcare industry, and ensures greater accountability. The HIPAA Privacy Rule provides federal protection for individually identifiable healthcare information held by covered facilities and their business associates. It also gives patients many rights concerning that information and permits the disclosure of information unless specified by the legislation. The Security Rule of HIPAA specifies a series of physical, administrative, and technical safeguards for facilities and their business associates to use for the purpose of confidentiality, availability, and integrity of electronic protected healthcare information (Muller, 2008).

12. **C.**

With workers' compensation laws, an employee who becomes ill, or is injured on the job or from a condition caused by the worksite, is compensated for that incident. Workers' compensation acts are state statutes, which establish liability of employers for injuries or illnesses to or of workers on the job due to the employment The Equal Employment Opportunity Commission (EEOC) enforces Title VII of the Civil Rights Act of 1964, the Age Discrimination in Employment Act of 1967 (ADEA), and Rehabilitation Act of 1973 ((Rundio & Wilson, 2010; U.S. Equal Employment Opportunity Commission, 2013a).

13. **B.**

Employers with 11 or more employees must keep records of work-related illnesses and injuries. This encompasses around 1.5 million companies and organizations or 20% of the establishments covered by OSHA. Workplaces that are exempt from record-keeping include low-hazard industries, such as finance, retail, insurance, real estate, and service (OSHA, 2013c).

14. **A.**

While laziness and poor supervision could contribute to failure to provide reasonable care, this is an example of negligence. With legal malpractice, there are four elements that apply: duty, breach, cause, and harm. All of these elements must be proven for a lawsuit to be successful (Muller, 2008).

15. **B.**

The Rehabilitation Act of 1973 ensures that qualified individuals with handicaps are not excluded from participation in various programs and activities or denied benefits from the employer. This regulation prohibits the discrimination against an employee with a disability who is otherwise qualified. A qualified handicapped person is someone who can perform the main functions of the job with reasonable accommodations (U.S. Equal Opportunity Commission, 2013b).

16. **C.**

The Equal Employment Opportunity Commission (EEOC) enforces Title VII of the Civil Rights Act of 1964, the Age Discrimination in Employment Act of 1967 (ADEA), and Rehabilitation Act of 1973. Equal employment laws involve various aspects of discrimination due to color, race, religion, age, national origin, sex, pregnancy, sexual orientation, and sexual harassment. The EEOC governs the act's interpretation and settles disputes regarding discrimination. This organization attempts to reach an agreement between the employee and employer through persuasion and conciliation (U.S. Equal Employment Opportunity Commission, 2013a). The Occupational Safety and Health Administration (OSHA) covers any employer who operates or engages in a business that affects commerce. The Alliance Program and the Safety and Health Achievement Recognition Program are both programs governed by OSHA (OSHA, 2013a; OSHA, 2013d).

17. **B.**

Civil law applies to the private rights of a person, whereas criminal law deals with crimes and their prosecution. A tort is a civil wrong, whereas a crime is a public wrong. Legal issues that affect case management involve healthcare provider licensure, quality care services, and various rules and regulations. Intentional and unintentional torts include assault, battery, trespass, and false imprisonment (Muller, 2008).

18. **D.**

Intentional torts include assault, battery, trespass, and false imprisonment. Informed consent is an example of a knowing and voluntary waiver of personal rights in the healthcare setting. Without this document, there is no waiver of rights, and the healthcare provider can be liable for assault, battery, or false imprisonment (Muller, 2008).

19. **A.**

Regarding RM and QI, both attempt to identify risk patterns and avoid adverse patient outcomes. Also, both involve monitoring trends in order to identify risk problems or patterns, both require cooperation from the multidisciplinary team, both uses similar tools and techniques to identify and resolve problematic issues, and both require complete and clear documentation (Powell & Tahan, 2010).

20. **A.**

RM investigates patient and visitor safety, environment, and exposures, whereas QI investigates patient-care-focused issues, such as optimal quality of care and adherence to professional standards. RM attempts to decrease adverse patient outcomes, whereas QI aims to increase quality patient outcomes. RM focuses on loss prevention, whereas QI assists with the enhancement of care and associated quality outcomes (Powell & Tahan, 2010).

21. **B.**

Level I involves an identified quality problem with minimal potential for adverse effects on the patient. An example is a patient discharged with mild hematuria without a follow-up plan. Level II involves an identified quality problem with significant potential for adverse effects on the patient. An example is the wrong intravenous medication was given, but the infusion was stopped before any harm occurred. Level III involves an identified quality problem with significant deviation from acceptable levels of care, and it resulted in injury or harm to the patient. An example is the loss of a limb or death related to poor medical/nursing care. There is no Level IV (Powell & Tahan, 2010).

22. **B.**

The process for identifying, investigating, reporting, and correcting APOs is called root cause analysis (RCA). Most RCA processes include a study of the environment where the APO occurred, identification of the personnel, equipment, and actions that were associated with the event, verification of the involved variables, and frequency of causes ranking (Powell & Tahan, 2010).

23. **D.**

An incident is an error, accident, or the discovery of a hazardous condition that is not consistent with quality standards of care or practice. A potentially compensable event is one that could result in litigation. Variances are deviations from expected and acceptable care. The incident report is a communication tool used to record all of these things. This document is used by RM personnel to assess for potential liabilities, document existing problems, and show the need for policy and procedure revision (Powell & Tahan, 2010).

24. **C.**

Clinical outcome measures = Morbidity rates, complication rates, and mortality rates. Utilization outcome measures = denial rate, appeals conversion rate, and surgical delays. Transitional planning outcome measures = return to operating room, return to intensive care unit, and readmission within 1 week of discharge. Cost outcome measures = length of stay, cost per day, and cost per case (Powell & Tahan, 2010).

25. **A.**

Core measures are set by the Centers for Medicare & Medicaid Services (CMS). These criteria are national standardized performance measurements that are used to improve the quality of care. The CMS system is often referred to as National Quality Measures. The core measures include: measures related to myocardial infarction care, heart failure care, pneumonia care, surgical infection prevention, and asthma care for children (Powell & Tahan, 2010).

26. **D.**

According to the U.S. Department of Health and Human Services (2013), oxygenation assessment, pneumococcal vaccination, and initial antibiotic within 4 hours of arrival are all three examples of core measures for a patient with pneumonia.

27. **B.**

The CMSA specifies the standards of practice for case managers, which are considered "performance indicators" and are essential elements in case management practice, education, and training. These include quality care, qualifications for case managers, collaboration with healthcare providers and patients, and several legal and ethical considerations (Stanton & Tahan, 2008). The four elements that apply to malpractice are duty, breach, cause, and harm (Muller, 2008). Quality indicators include core measures and case management outcome indicators. The Code of Professional Conduct for Case Managers requires case managers to adhere to five principles of professional conduct: autonomy, beneficence, non-maleficence, justice, and veracity (Powell & Tahan, 2010).

28. **D.**

Standard A: Patient Selection Process for Case Management – The case manager should identify and select clients who can most benefit from case management services available in a particular practice setting. Standard B: Patient Assessment – The case manager should complete a health and psychosocial assessment, taking into account the cultural and linguistic needs of each client. Standard C:

Problem/Opportunity Identification – The case manager should identify problems or opportunities that would benefit from case management intervention. Standard D: Planning –The case manager should identify immediate, short-term, long-term, and ongoing needs, as well as develop appropriate and necessary case management strategies and goals to address those needs (Case Management Society of America, 2010).

29. **D.**

Core measures for pediatric asthma include immediate relievers, systemic corticosteroid, and a home management plan of care. Prophylactic antibiotic within 1 hour before, appropriate hair removal, and appropriate thromboembolism prophylaxis are all core measures for surgical infection prevention (U.S. Department of Health and Human Services, 2013).

30. **C.**

Standard K: Ethics – Case managers should behave and practice ethically, adhering to the tenets of the code of ethics that underlies his/her professional credential (e.g., nursing, social work, rehabilitation counseling, etc.). Standard L: Advocacy – The case manager should advocate for the client at the service-delivery, benefits-administration, and policy-making levels. Standard M: Cultural Competency – The case manager should be aware of, and responsive to, cultural and demographic diversity of the population and specific client profiles. Standard N: Resource Management and Stewardship – The case manager should integrate factors related to quality, safety, access, and cost-effectiveness in assessing, monitoring, and evaluating resources for the client's care (Case Management Society of America, 2010).

31. **B.**

Standard E: Monitoring – The case manager should employ ongoing assessment and documentation to measure the client's response to the plan of care. Standard F: Outcomes – The case manager should maximize the client's health, wellness, safety, adaptation, and self-care through quality case management, client satisfaction, and cost-efficiency. Standard G: Termination of Case Management Services – The case manager should appropriately terminate case management services based upon CMSA Standards of Practice for Case Management. Standard H: Facilitation, Coordination, and Collaboration – The case manager should facilitate coordination, communication, and collaboration with the client and other stakeholders in order to achieve goals and maximize positive client outcomes (Case Management Society of America, 2010).

32. **D.**

According to Powell & Tahan (2010), variance outcome measures are system-, community-, and practitioner-related.

33. **B.**

The CCMC's Code of Professional Conduct for Case Managers is the ethical code of the profession, and case managers should review this code and standards regularly and work within the case management scope of practice, which includes adherence to professional guidelines and job descriptions (Banja, 2008).

34. **C.**

According to the FLSA Child Labor Provisions, the basic minimum age for employment is 16 years. However, employment of 14- and 15-year-old youths is allowed for certain occupations and under specific guidelines (Rundio & Wilson, 2010).

Psychosocial Aspects (20%)

1. **D.**

Child abuse has many variations and exists in all ethnic and socioeconomic groups. Child abuse reporting is mandatory in all states. If a classic case is not reported, healthcare providers who are involved in the child's care can be charged criminally and found negligent. Child abuse includes non-accidental injuries, exploitation, and sexual abuse (Muller, 2010).

2. **D.**

Psychosocial evaluation of patients should involve an assessment of their value systems, traditions, and beliefs (Powell & Tahan, 2010).

3. **D.**

Poverty is a risk factor for malnutrition because many individuals cannot afford to purchase nutritious foods. Other risk factors for malnutrition include a recent weight gain or loss of ten pounds or more, ill-fitting dentures, lack of teen, dental caries, tooth abscesses, living alone, and a history of eating disorders.

4. **C.**

Patients who experience an unintentional overdose should be referred for a psychosocial evaluation because the overdose could have occurred from inability to read instructions, polypharmacy, excessive use of medications, and/or lack of knowledge. Other indications for a psychosocial evaluation include chronic mental illness, eating disorders, substance abuse, intentional overdose, and dementia. Heart diseases, single status, and limited financial sources do not readily indicate the need for a psychosocial evaluation.

5. **D.**

Bereavement is the time period of mourning. The amount of time varies from person to person, but typically is 6-12 months or longer. Grief is a normal response to loss and mourning is the public expression of grief. The three types of grief are acute, chronic, and anticipatory. With chronic grief, the person is at risk for depression, which is characterized by feelings of sadness and changes in mood (Wraa, Coulter, & Kelly, 2010).

6. **C.**

For some cultures, the spiritual belief system is a major source of strength. There are numerous religious and dietary practices to consider. Jehovah's Witness members do not believe in blood transfusions, which can alter the treatment plan and create ethical concerns (Powell & Tahan, 2010).

7. **B.**

When it comes to belief about health, culture is a major contributing factor. In many non-Western cultures, people believe that illness comes from natural or unnatural causes. The natural causes that some believe contribute to health problems include heat, cold, dampness, and wind. Therefore, the person may not consider that medicines would affect their health status. Unnatural causes that are thought to contribute to illness include spirits, supernatural forces, or deities (Wraa, Coulter, & Kelly, 2010).

8. **B.**

High-volume users of behavioral health case management services are people with severe and persistent mental illness (SPMI), which is a diagnosis of nonorganic psychosis of personality disorder. A SPMI is characterized as prolonged illness, which often requires long-term treatment and results in disability (Rosedale & Bigio, 2008).

9. **E.**

With the Brokerage Model, a case manager coordinates care among all involved parties. This model has an extended form, where leadership is assumed by mental health professionals who are actively involved in the patient's care. A psychiatrist is often the leader of the interdisciplinary team. This model is designed to provide services for individuals with SPMIs. The functions of the case manager include patient advocacy, transportation of consumers to and from treatment sites, symptom and medication monitoring, assessment and teaching regarding community living, and initiating and coordinating referrals, benefits, and entitlements (Rosedale & Bigio, 2008).

10. **A.**

The Strengths Model differs from the Brokerage Model in that most services are provided outside an office setting. Staff services include broad areas of engagement, which includes identification of achievements, aspirations and interests of the patient, sensitivity to patient's preferences, and use of case manager's self-disclosure; personal planning, which focuses on the measurable steps made toward achieving what the patient desires; strengths assessment, which involves prioritizing the patient's past and present accomplishments, resources, and future interests; and resource acquisition, which requires designing activities with the patient to increase contact with community resources (Rosedale & Bigio, 2008).

11. **C.**

The Assertive Community Treatment (ACT) Model is the most recognized and articulate mode used by case managers and healthcare facilities. Research shows that this model controls psychiatric symptoms, reduces hospital use, increases housing stability, and improves quality of life (Rosedale & Bigio, 2008).

12. **A.**

The Pain Assessment in Advanced Dementia (PAINAD) scale – This tool utilizes careful observation of non-verbal behavior to evaluate pain. Changes are noted in vocalization, which includes moaning, negative speech, absent speech, and crying, respirations, which involves rapid and labored breathing with short periods of Cheyne-Stokes or hyperventilation, body language, which involves tension, fidgeting, clenching fists, pacing, and lying in a fetal position, and consolability, where the patient is less easily distractible or not consolable.

13. **A.**

The Mini-Cog test assesses for dementia with two components: drawing the face of a clock with all 12 numbers and hands in order to show the time specified and repeating the names of three common objects that are given early in the interview process.

14. **D.**

Religion and spirituality may plan a major role in a patient's terminally ill experience and how that person responds to the dying process. Assessing the role of spiritual or religious beliefs is an important component of the psychosocial assessment and should take place as early as possible in the palliative care case manager-patient relationship. Some patients do not identify strongly with religious or spiritual beliefs and should not be urged to do this (Wraa, Coulter, & Kelly, 2010).

15. **B.**

With the brick wall syndrome, a psychosocial situation occurs where a patient requires intensive care, and family member insist that they can provide this at home. When the family members "hit the brick wall," they realize that they are unable to care for the patient in the home setting and request a long-term care facility. When the case manager suspects that home placement will not succeed, he or she should make necessary preparations for placement of the patient just in case it is needed (Wraa, Coulter, & Kelly, 2010).

16. **C.**

People with alcohol abuse also show a maladaptive pattern of alcohol consumption that results in adverse consequences during a twelve-month time period. For both narcotics and alcohol abuse, these consequences include recurrent substance use in situations where it can be hazardous, such as driving, failure to fulfill role obligations at school, work, or home, such as repeated absences, recurrent use-related legal problems, such as disorderly conduct arrest, and continued use of substance despite social and interpersonal problems that it causes, such as divorce or altercations (Rosedale & Bigio, 2008).

17. **E.**

Several indicators need to be evaluated and addressed concerning the family of the technology-dependent or medically fragile child. Family members often experience adverse consequences when a child has a chronic condition. Indicators of child health outcomes include income, employment, parental health, sibling health, sibling adaption, family interaction, and family support (Davis, 2008).

18. **D.**

Intravenous hydration is considered a medical intervention in the U.S., so it can be refused if the patient or family feels it is a burden. The administration of intravenous hydration to a dying patient should be determined based on the patient's goals and symptoms. Family members and caregivers often find it emotionally difficult to not provide hydration to a dying person. Dehydration can often lead to improvement with certain symptoms associated with the dying process, such as edema, vomiting, and respiratory congestion (Wraa, Coulter, & Kelly, 2010).

19. **D.**

During the dying process, the terminally ill patient often lacks the mental capacity to make end-of-life treatment decisions. Family members often become the primary medical decision-makers in the absence of a durable power of attorney. Many conflicts arise concerning the dying process, due to varying values and opinions among the family members. Members of the palliative care team should encourage family members to do what they believe the patient would have wanted for him or herself if he or she was able to make these decisions (Wraa, Coulter, & Kelly, 2010).

20. **D.**

When a child is sick, each member of the family is affected to some degree. Many family units are blended, whereas others are extended. The case manager must establish the primary caregiver, which if usually the child's mother or father. The primary caregiver is the one who is responsible for learning all aspects of the child's care. The case manager needs to assess the caregiver's readiness and willingness to learn, as well as the motivation level and ability to learn (Davis, 2008).

21. **B.**

Local public health departments can provide in-home visits by public health nurses for activities associated with health promotion The American Association of Retired Persons (AARP) has information on every aspect of aging and is a resource for case managers and patients. The Area Agency on Aging (AAA) offers a variety of programs, including referral to hands-on support programs. The American Society on Aging sponsors conferences for case managers and other healthcare providers to attend. Services organizations, such as the Salvation Army and the St. Vincent DePaul Society, offer programs for the elderly, such as friendly visitor programs, adult day health programs, free or low-cost transportation, and equipment loan programs (Alvarado & Sunderland, 2008).

22. **D.**

To increase the mother's support system, the case manager must coordinate patient education efforts. Prenatal classes are offered by many healthcare facilities and nonprofit organizations. Also, Lamaze classes should be encouraged. Many HMOs offer educational programs for new mothers and prenatal screening for pregnant women. These programs offer information materials, such as booklets, tapes, brochures, and books. Many HMO programs offer incentives to their plan participants for early prenatal care, bimonthly visits, and/or participation in a perinatal wellness program (Davis, 2008).

23. **D.**

Poverty causes many challenges to the provision of optimal palliative care for the terminally ill and dying patient. Many patients who live in poverty have unstable or nonexistent housing, making "home" care quite difficult. The lack of dependable transportation can cause trouble with getting to scheduled medical visits or urgent care services. Also, patients who live in poverty often do not have basic needs, such as shelter, food, and a stable support system. However, patients living in poverty do not always have less effective coping skills. As with other socioeconomic groups, these patients have a wide range of psychological reactions to the dying process and end-of-life issues. Many patients who struggle to meet basic human needs are flexible, resilient, and pragmatic when faced with challenges (Wraa, Coulter, & Kelly, 2010).

24. **B.**

An unwanted or unplanned pregnancy can constitute a situational crisis in which the problem leads to disruption of normal psychological functioning. Other examples of situational crisis include divorce, death of a loved one, onset or change in a disease process, loss of job or career, and being a victim of a violent act. Community situational crises are events that affect an entire community. These include terrorist attacks, floods, hurricanes, earthquakes, and tornadoes (Rittenmyer, 2010).

25. **C.**

The CAGE assessment tool assesses for abuse of alcohol. The "C" indicates "cutting down," the "A" indicates "annoyed at criticism," the "G" indicates "guilty feelings," and the "E" indicates "eye opener." Answering "yes" to one question on the CAGE questionnaire suggest the possibility of a drinking problem, and answering "yes" on two or more of these questions indicates and actual drinking problem (Trigoboff, 2010).

26. **D.**

Psychological abuse involves intimidation measures and threats. His occurs when caregivers make frequent threats to hit the person and using intimidation with a weapon when the person does not cooperate. Psychological abuse makes the patient feel anxious and terrified Neglect is failure to provide basic needs, and it can be intentional (active) or unintentional (inactive). Financial abuse includes staling, fraud, and forcing people to sign away property. Physical abuse involves various types of assaults, such as biting, hitting, pulling hair, kicking, pushing, and shoving (Rittenmeyer, 2010).

27. **A.**

An indication of financial abuse is the disappearance of items from the home. Family, caregivers, and friends often take one or two items at time, assuming that the person will not notice. Other forms of financial abuse include forcing a patient to sign over property, outright stealing of property, persuading patients to turn over possessions, using stolen credit cards, emptying bank accounts, convincing the person to invest money in a fraudulent scheme, and taking money for home renovations that do not get done (Rittenmeyer, 2010).

28. **C.**

A patient or parent's refusal of care can be overridden in a few specific instances. These include when the patient is mentally incompetent to make decisions even though advance directives were established prior to the onset of dementia, and when refusing care puts the general public at risk, such as with treatment for highly communicable diseases (Rittenmeyer, 2010).

29. **B.**

Jung's theory is called the Theory of Individualism. This theory holds that one's personality continues to develop during the course of a lifespan. Personality comprises personal unconsciousness, collective unconsciousness, and ego. Also, personality is both introverted and extroverted, with a balance needed for adequate emotional health. Jung proposed that during middle age, people begin to question their beliefs, values, and attainments and turn inward as they continue to age. Successful aging involves value of oneself more than the concern for external things, physical limitations, and losses (Rittenmeyer, 2010).

30. **B.**

In this situation, it is most appropriate to refer the single mother to a social worker who has the expertise to require assistance of this nature. Social workers can assist patients with such programs as Temporary Assistance for Needy Families (TANF) and food stamps. Also, the social worker can help the patient avoid homelessness by assisting with subsidized and low-cost housing (Rittenmeyer, 2010).

31. **D.**

The durable power of attorney is a legal document that designates a person to make decisions regarding all medical and end-of-life care when a patient is mentally incompetent. This document is a type of advance directive, which also includes specific requests of the patient regarding treatment and living wills. A DNR order is a document that indicates the patient does not want to be resuscitated for a terminal condition or illness. A general power of attorney allows one designated person to make broad decisions for the patient (Wraa, Coulter, & Kelly, 2010).

32. **A.**

The first step in a cultural assessment is to establish trust by respecting the patient's cultural values and traditions, making careful observations, and listening to the patient's concerns. Cultural assessment is part of a psychosocial evaluation, so asking permission and explaining the purpose of this is not necessary. For some ethnic groups, taking notes while talking is considered rude, so the case manager should explain the purpose or the notes and maintain focus on the patient and family instead of paperwork (Rittenmeyer, 2010).

33. **D.**

Palliative care begins when the patient is diagnosed with a life-threatening disease or terminal illness, such as advanced cancer or end-stage renal disease. Many patients are referred to palliative care when they have serious chronic diseases even though death does not appear imminent. The patient's request alone for this service is not adequate without the proper diagnosis. Also, palliative care is often supportive in the early stages but will intensify as the patient's condition deteriorates (Wraa, Coulter, & Kelly, 2010).

34. **D.**

Depression among elderly patients occurs with many conditions that decrease quality of life, such as arthritis, cancer, neuromuscular diseases, stroke, heart disease, diabetes, and Huntington's disease. Many drugs can precipitate depression, such as cimetidine, hydralazine, corticosteroids, Parkinson's drugs, diuretics, propranolol, and digitalis. Symptoms of depression include changes in appetite, increased fatigue, sadness, loss of interest in usual activities, sadness, anxiety, and sleep disturbances (Rittenmeyer, 2010).

35. **B.**

Dual diagnosis is the term that refers to combined substance abuse and a mental health disorder. The initial treatment for a dual diagnosis involves detoxification from drugs so the mental health condition can be accurately assessed. After detoxification, the patient undergoes rehabilitation and mental health treatment, which involves the use of medications and/or therapy (Trigoboff, 2010).

Healthcare Management and Delivery (20%)

1. **C.**
Medical units most often require the services of a case manager. Medical patients usually are older people who have complex discharge plans. These patients are not as able to advocate for themselves, so they often fall through the cracks during and after an extended hospital stay. Each medical unit case manager typically has an average caseload of 20 to 25 patients (Cohen & Cesta, 2005).

2. **D.**
The case management plan in an ambulatory or outpatient facility is developed based on each patient's expected outcomes. This approach is often used for clinic visits, home care visits, outpatient surgery visits, and urgent care visits (Cohen & Cesta, 2005).

3. **B.**
Surgical unit patients are often complicated, but their hospital course is more predictable and amendable to a predetermined plan than medical patients. Criteria for patient selection on the surgical unit are based on patient need, case complexity, and severity of illness or condition (Cohen & Cesta, 2005).

4. **A.**
Sub-acute care is a level of care that blends long-term care and acute care skills and philosophies. Sub-acute care facilities often bridge acute and long-term care, and the patient stay is shorter than with a skilled nursing facility. Most patients are admitted to these facilities following a hospitalization, and models include short-term medically complex, short-term rehabilitative, and chronic (Cohen & Cesta, 2005).

5. **B.**
Disease management (DM) is a system of coordinated healthcare interventions and communications for patients of a certain population and who have conditions in which patient self-care efforts are similar. A Disease Management Model is a holistic care model in which all components work toward the good of the patients of a particular population (Powell & Tahan, 2008).

6. **C.**
In the disease management process, evaluation of outcome measures involves the use clinical and quality indicators to assess outcomes and use cost indicators to assess financial outcomes (Powell & Tahan, 2008).

7. **D.**
The disposition of the patient at discharge is called the discharge status, and it indicates what level of care the patient is going to receive. The discharge status indicates how the healthcare facility will be paid using specific codes assigned to various dispositions (Birmingham, 2008).

8. **A.**

   The disease management process involves: identification of at-risk patients by using criteria to assess high-risk patients for select diseases, assessment and evaluation of patients, which involves psychosocial issues, financial factors, competency barriers to self-care, disease-specific clinical details, and severity of target disease state (priority 1, 2 or 3), development of DM plans, by using evidence-based practice guidelines to establish goals and objectives, implement DM plans, which involves ongoing monitoring and assessment of the patient's condition, referrals to specialist as necessary, and involvement of the patient and family in the DM program, and evaluation of outcome measures by using clinical and quality indicators to assess outcomes, and use cost indicators to assess financial outcomes (Powell & Tahan, 2008).

9. **B.**

   Continuum of care is a concept that involves an integrated system of care to guide and track a patient over time through a comprehensive method that covers all levels of care. Common intervention tools include preventive screenings, risk assessment, risk reduction, and self-care education. Many measures focus on chronological patterns of care but do not directly measure continuity or any of the aspects of care associated with connection and coherence (Haggerty, Reid, Freeman, Starfield, & Adair, 2003).

10. **B.**

    Management continuity is facilitated by shared care protocols that provide a sense of security and predictability. One important aspect of this type of continuity is flexibility in adapting care to changes in the patient's circumstances and/or needs. This type of continuity is achieved when services are conducted in a timely and complementary manner (Haggerty, Reid, Freeman, Starfield, & Adair, 2003).

11. **A.**

    CMS developed the Conditions of Participation (CoP), which are standards that healthcare facilities must meet in order to participate in government insurance programs. These standards improve quality and protect the safety and well-being of health plan members. The CoP standards apply to patients receiving services regarding discharge planning, medical records, and patients' rights (Birmingham, 2008).

12. **C.**

    While the interdisciplinary team members work closely and communicate frequently to promote patient care, the multidisciplinary team members work in parallel to each other with little communication. With a trans-disciplinary team, the team members operate at the opposite end of the continuum, professional functions overlap, and roles of the individual team members are blurred (Hall & Weaver, 2001).

13. **A.**

In order for the insurance company to cover rehabilitation services and treatment, there are two fundamental requirements that must be met. These are: the care must be reasonable and necessary as related to duration, frequency, efficacy, and amount, and the care must be reasonable and necessary to provide the care in an inpatient setting, rather than in a less-intensive facility (Schoenbeck, Tahan, & Powell, 2008).

14. **B.**

Structured in a yes/no method, algorithms are schematic models that support the use of clinical decision pathways. The decision points of an algorithm depend on specific characteristic and/or diagnostic and treatment options. These simple decision trees are useful clinical tools that do not account for all patient-related variables. Rather, they are intended to be used as guides for clinical settings, disease states, economic issues, and insurance purposes (McKendry, 2008).

15. **C.**

The National Committee for Quality Assurance (NCQA) Physician Practice Connections and Patient Centered Medical Home (PPC-PCMH) Recognition Program developed the medical home model in 2003, with the support from many professional organizations (National Committee on Quality Assurance, 2013).

16. **B.**

For an organization or facility to achieve PCMH Recognition, specific elements must be met. With Element 4B (self-management support), the practice works to facilitate self-management of care for patients with one of the three clinically important conditions (National Committee on Quality Assurance, 2013).

17. **D.**

With palliative care case management, care and services are given by an interdisciplinary team and coordinated by a case manager (Correoso & Santiago, 2008).

18. **B.**

Ejection fraction < 20%, arrhythmias resistant to treatment, and discomfort with physical activity are examples of heart disease indicators. Physical decline, weight loss, and multiple comorbidities are examples of core indicators. PT > 5 seconds, ascites resistant to treatment, and hepatorenal syndrome are examples of liver disease indicators. Intractable fluid overload, oliguria < 40 cc/24 hours, and hyperkalemia are renal disease indicators (Correoso & Santiago, 2008).

19. **B.**

Rehabilitation services are provided in acute care hospitals, rehabilitation centers, sub-acute care facilities, long-term care facilities, comprehensive outpatient rehabilitation facilities (CORFs), day rehabilitation services (DRSs), and home rehabilitation through home health agencies (Schoenbeck, Tahan, & Powell, 2008).

20. **C.**

There are many healthcare providers who participate with the interdisciplinary team to provide rehabilitation services. The team sets both short- and long-term treatment goals for the patient. The team members include a physiatrist who specializes in rehabilitation and physical medicine (Schoenbeck, Tahan, & Powell, 2008).

21. **B.**

Discharge planning is a process of assessing a patient's needs after discharge from a healthcare facility and putting the necessary services in place before discharge. The case manager will ensure a safe discharge to the next level of care or setting, provide appropriate resources for ongoing care, and ensure a timely and safe transition (Birmingham, 2008).

22. **D.**

The four components of a critical pathway include a timeline, identified care categories and/or activities and their interventions, outcome criteria, including immediate, intermediate, and long-term, and allowance for deviations and variances (McKendry, 2008).

23. **B.**

Code 01-Discharged to home (routine discharge) indicates discharge to home on oxygen or with DME services without the need for residential care or home health. Code 02-Discharged to a short-term healthcare facility indicates same-day transfer for an inpatient claim. Code 04-Discharged to an intermediate care facility (ICF) indicates that requires nursing care in state-designated assisted living facility (Centers for Medicare & Medicaid Services, 2005).

24. **B.**

Critical pathways are healthcare provider documents that detail the main elements of day-to-day care activities necessary for a typical patient with a specific diagnosis. These tools are created to show current practice parameters and/or recommended "best practices." Critical pathways show target lengths of stay and anticipated levels of care, and they incorporate interdisciplinary teams (McKendry, 2008).

25. **D.**

The Chronic Care Model was created to address deficiencies in chronic care, as well as the aging population and number of patients with chronic conditions, and it can be applied to many chronic illnesses and in a variety of healthcare settings. The goal of the model is healthier patients, satisfied providers, and cost savings. This model identifies several essential elements of a healthcare system that promotes high-quality chronic disease management and care, including community, healthcare system, self-management support, delivery system design, decisions support, and clinical information systems (Improving Chronic Illness Care, 2013).

26. **B.**

Both sub-acute and rehabilitation facilities provide intravenous care that can include multiple medications and infusion pumps. These facilities offer monitoring by RNs who manage complex drug regimens. Also, they provide care for patients on ventilators or those who require endotracheal suctioning (Birmingham, 2008).

27. **C.**

The Milliman Care Guidelines are now called the General Recovery Care Guidelines. They cover a wide range of topics for various levels of patient care. General recovery guidelines are used with patients who have complex medical situations that do not fit into other guidelines (Milliman Care Guidelines, 2013).

28. **A.**

Also called handover, handoff of a patient from one level is part of transition of care. This may occur within the healthcare facility when a patient transfers from one unit to another or between two facilities. Transition of care also involves a change in the plan of acre or health plan (Birmingham, 2008).

29. **D.**

For reintegration into the community, a patient who has suffered a serious injury or illness requires a comprehensive plan of care. Issues addressed in this plan include financial support, job training, housing, family support, medical assistance, assistive technology, environmental modifications, follow-up and continued services, and safety. The goals for reintegration must be realistic and have timeframes based on patient's activities and skills. The case manager must be aware of all necessary services, available resources, and needed referrals (Birmingham, 2008).

30. **C.**

Collaboration among members of the interdisciplinary team requires open sharing of ideals and perspectives in order to solve problems. Open sharing and respect for others is necessary for this collaboration. Cost saving, time saving, and improved patient satisfaction all tend to result from innovative approaches to problem-solving (Hall & Weaver, 2001).

31. **C.**

Because an IQ of 70 is considered mild retardation, the best place for this patient would be a group home. In these facilities, the patient can usually manage self-care with minimal supervision. These licensed facilities usually house four to eight patients with similar conditions and illnesses (Birmingham, 2008).

32. **B.**

In order to facilitate the continuum of care after a patient is discharged from an acute care facility, the case manager should establish relationships with staff of skilled nursing facilities and home health agencies, as well as sub-acute care facilities, rehabilitation centers, and assisted living facilities (Birmingham, 2008).

33. **C.**

With a trans-disciplinary team, the team members operate at the opposite end of the continuum, professional functions overlap, and roles of the individual team members are blurred (Hall & Weaver, 2001).

34. **A.**

One disease management option is the Component Management Model of healthcare, which involves numerous providers who are the "components" along the continuum. Disease management can support education and preventive care to reduce hospitalizations and emergency care visits (Powell & Tahan, 2008).

35. **A.**

Most patients are admitted to rehabilitation facilities following a hospitalization, and models used include short-term medically complex, short-term rehabilitative, and chronic. Short-term medically complex patients are typically postsurgical patients or those who have complex medical conditions but are stable. Short-term rehabilitative patients are those who have potential for improvement, but still have significant nursing needs and are unable to tolerate intense rehabilitation. Chronic care patients have an extended acute care stay, are medically stable, and require high ancillary and/or nursing care needs (Cohen & Cesta, 2005).

Healthcare Reimbursement (15%)

1. **B.**

APGs are DRGs in the ambulatory setting that are used to reimburse the cost of providing outpatient procedures or visits, and they do not cover the physician cost elements. The ambulatory payment classification (APC) is a more refined reimbursement strategy that CMS implemented, which attempts to predict the amount and type of resources used for various ambulatory visits. PPS rates reimburse for ancillary, routine, and capital-related costs (Cohen & Cesta, 2005).

2. **C.**

For skilled nursing facilities, resource utilization groups (RUGs) use the minimum data set (MDS) to differentiate nursing home patients by their levels of resource use. With this, PPS rates reimburse for ancillary, routine, and capital-related costs (Cohen & Cesta, 2005).

3. **B.**

The case manager often facilitates hard savings such as change in level of care, length of stay, and contracted PPO provider, as well as negotiation of price of services, equipment, supplies, per diem rates, frequency of services, and duration of services. Soft savings are potential costs or charges that are less tangibly measurable than hard savings, which represents costs that are bypassed with case management intervention. Examples include avoidance of potential hospital readmissions, medical complications, acute care days, legal exposure, emergency department visits, and added costs, supplies, and equipment (Powell, 2008).

4. **D.**

Costs can be contained through a process called reduction in force (RIF). Strategies of RIF include the cutback or elimination of services that are not critical to the healthcare facility's goals regarding financial viability (Rundio & Wilson, 2010).

5. **A.**

Clinical variables affect length of stay include urgent of emergent patient status, poor health status of patient, concomitant levels of severity of primary diagnosis, comorbidity and complications, discharge planning, timely social service planning, and nursing case management model (Cohen & Cesta, 2005).

6. **B.**

The cost-effectiveness analysis (CEA) method is one economic process used to evaluate outcomes and costs of treatments and interventions or delivery systems. CEA is a method for evaluating and monitoring resource costs and health outcomes of patient care, and its central function is to demonstrate the relative value of alternative interventions (Tahan, 2005c).

7. **B.**

The case management quality index (CMQI) score is calculated based on the unit of analysis identified in the CEA study. It can include the patient care environment. Average cost per patient is calculated by dividing the total costs per environment accrued in a specific time period by the total number of patient s cared for in that environment in that same time period. Calculation of cost-effectiveness ratio is a measure of case management value. A low C/E ratio is desirable because this indicates better outcomes and less costs. A high C/E ratio is associated with lower value (Tahan, 2005).

8. **D.**

The types of costs (used or considered) are derived from an analytical perspective. Examples of costs include costs of services (utilization reviews, equipment, and communication method), cost of case managers (salaries and benefits), and costs of equipment and supplies (computers, machines, and paperwork) (Tahan, 2005c).

9. **B.**

Capitation is a set amount paid to the healthcare provider on the basis of per member per year or per month, regardless of services provided. Co-pay is a predetermined dollar amount for which a health plan member must pay at the time a service is rendered. Deductible refers to a fixed amount of money a health plan member must pay each year before benefits are paid by the insurance company (Powell & Tahan, 2010).

10. **A.**

Prospective review, also called preadmission review, is completed by a representative from the healthcare provider agency in order to decide whether the admission of a patient to an inpatient facility is justified or not. The review occurs before services are rendered, and the reviewer decides if or not the admission is medical necessary (Powell & Tahan, 2010).

11. **B.**

A concurrent review is performed while the patient is in the healthcare facility. UM reviewers conduct reviews via telephone, fax, or electronic mail. The reviewer determines level of care and communicates with the insurance company. Concurrent review involves admission review (performed within 24 hours of admission) and continued stay review (performed every two to three days) (Powell & Tahan, 2010).

12. **B.**

The out-of-pocket maximum is the maximum per calendar year for which a health plan member pays. Co-payments, co-insurance, and deductibles all go toward this maximum (Powell & Tahan, 2010).

13. **B.**

The reimbursement mechanism is the method applied for payment of services rendered. Examples include fee for service, case rate, capitated rate, discounted, and per diem (Cunningham, 2008).

14. **B.**

Risk sharing is the process where an HMO and healthcare provider both accept a portion of the responsibility for financial risk and awards (Cunningham, 2008).

15. **A.**

There are numerous nonclinical variables that affect length of stay and healthcare costs. These include the day of admission. Medical admissions on Sunday have lowest average length of stay, whereas medical admissions on Friday have the highest (Cohen & Cesta, 2005).

16. **C.**

Case management and interdepartmental coordination and integration of patient services decreased hospital length of stay. This is achieved by regular meetings among nursing service, laboratory personnel, and radiology personnel. Increased laboratory and radiology services are associated with longer length of stay (Cohen & Cesta, 2005).

17. **C.**

Prospective payment system in the home care setting is called home health resource groups (HHRGs), which involves reimbursement for home care services based on a nursing assessment done at the first home visit (Powell & Tahan, 2010).

18. **C.**

Exclusive Provider Organizations (EPOs) are structured much like PPOs, but they have a limitation with provider choice, and they are not subject to as many rigorous insurance laws as HMOs. Independent Practice Associations (IPAs) have independent physicians or small physician group practices that contract with one or more managed healthcare organizations. Direct Contract Model HMO contracts directly with individual physicians to provide all services to health plan members (Gerardi, 2005).

19. **A.**

There are five common models of health maintenance organizations (HMOs). With the Staff Model, the physicians are employed by the HMO to provide all services to health plan members. With the Group Practice Model, the HMO contracts multispecialty physician group practices to provide all services to the health plan members. With the Network Model, the HMO contracts with many group practices to provide all services to the health plan members. With the Independent Practice Association Model the HMO contracts an association of physicians to provide all services to health plan members (Gerardi, 2005).

20. **B.**

With per diem, organizations are paid a specific amount per day regardless of actual costs, and this is based on number of days of service and averaging costs. With discounted fee for service, providers are paid a set fee for a specific service, but at a previously set discounted rate. With fee for service, providers are paid a set fee for each service provided, and no discounts are given. With percent of charges, organizations are paid a fixed percentage of charges, based on the patient's bill and contractual agreements (Cunningham, 2008).

21. **B.**

According to Cunningham (2008), DRG case rate is the rate of reimbursement that covers a certain category of services. This usually combines healthcare provider and facility fees.

22. **D.**

With the utilization management review process, a customer service representative determines covered benefits by accessing the benefit plan, checking for covered services, and evaluating UM review requirements (Lattimer & Garrett, 2008).

23. **D.**

   According to Lattimer & Garrett (2008), utilization management program goals include: determine medical necessity and need for services; ensure proper utilization of healthcare resources through continuous evaluation; locate patterns of underutilization, overutilization, and poor use of resources; promote quality care and effective outcomes; provide education of the UM process to healthcare providers and hospital staff; locate cooperation of care options for members and providers; and identify disease management participants and case management programs.

24. **A.**

   The purpose of stop-loss insurance is to protect an insurance company against excessive payments. Stop-loss insurance is a form of reinsurance, which pays a percentage of bills over a certain covered amount. Stop-loss protects smaller self-funded insurance plans because the primary insurance typically covers the first $150,000 of medical bills, and the stop-loss insurance pays around 80% of the bills that are over than amount (Cunningham, 2008).

25. **C.**

   With Medicare, the benefit period begins on admission to an inpatient facility and ends after the patient has been discharged from the facility for 60 days. The benefit period includes the day of admission and the day of discharge. The first 60 days require no co-insurance but from days 61 to 90, the patient is responsible for a daily co-insurance charge. Hospital stay over 90 days requires the use of a lifetime reserve or another payment type. Patient soften have multiple benefit periods during a one year time period, but have to pay a deductible for each benefit period (Cunningham, 2008).

26. **A.**

   There are 25 major categories and 494 diagnoses involved with DRGs. There are numerous variables that determine the choice of diagnostic-related group (DRG) for a patient, such as primary diagnosis, secondary diagnosis, age, sex, complications, comorbidities, treatment procedures, discharge status, and length of stay. The DRG is scored based on its potential consumption and intensity of resources, and each DRG category has a specific acuity rating (also called the relative rate as well as an expected length of stay (Powell & Tahan, 2010).

27. **D.**

   Appeals for a denial of urgent care services must be decided by the insurance company within 72 hours. Insurance companies have 30 days to make a decision regarding non-urgent care that the patient is waiting to receive. A patient can appeal directly to the insurance company if care is ruled medically unnecessary or denied for some other purpose. Other common reasons for denial include experimental treatment, preexisting condition that is not covered, and the patient is not eligible for the service (Gerardi, 2005).

Rehabilitation (5%)

1. **D.**
   Rehabilitation care and services meet the needs of people with impairments, disabilities, or handicaps. Vocational skills involve work-related activities. Self-care skills include activities of daily living, such as bathing, feeding, and dressing. Mobility skills include walking, transferring, and use of wheelchair. Communication skills include speech, writing, and alternative methods of communication. Cognitive skills include memory, judgment, concentration, and problem-solving. Socialization skills include interacting with others in the community (Schoenbeck, Tahan, & Powell, 2008).

2. **B.**
   Comprehensive outpatient rehabilitation facilities (CORFs) deliver OT, PT, and ST, as well as prosthetic and orthotic devices and durable medical equipment (DME) on an outpatient basis. Individuals who utilize CORFs must be mobile and active. Medicare Part B covers $1,500 per year on outpatient PT/OT services. Intermediate rehabilitation facilities (IRFs) are free-standing hospitals or units that provide intensive rehabilitation services and care. Skilled nursing facilities (SNFs) and long-term care facilities (LTCs) are sub-acute rehabilitation facilities that provide care to patients who no longer require intensive hospital care but have a need for rehabilitation (Schoenbeck, Tahan, & Powell, 2008).

3. **B.**
   In many skilled nursing facilities, 30% of the charges are for rehabilitation services (Powell & Tahan, 2010).

4. **C.**
   Medicare assists with payment for medically necessary outpatient occupational therapy (OT), physical therapy (PT), and speech therapy (ST) services if the physician or therapist sets up the plan and the physician periodically reviews that plan for patient progression and addition need for services (Powell & Tahan, 2010).

5. **A.**
   Work hardening is an interdisciplinary, job-specific concept that involves activity with the goal of return-to-work, and it provides a transition between acute care and successful return-to-work. Work hardening programs are individualized and use real or simulated work tasks and conditioning exercises that are based on the injured person's measured tolerances (Washington State Department of Labor & Industries, 2013).

6. **C.**
   Workforce management involves work adjustment, work transition, and work hardening. The concept of workforce management involves all aspects of occupational disability and proactive health and safety information and training, as

well as non-occupational lost-time cases and effective return-to-work status. Workforce management includes benefit plan design, demographics of the employer's worker populations, health and productivity programs, and integration of benefit programs, such as integrated disability management and occupational case management (Provine & Vierling, 2008).

7. **B.**

Workers' compensation laws were developed by federal statute in 1908, but they are enforced on the state level. Workers' compensation varies from state to state, but it is designed to provide medical and compensatory benefits to employees who are hurt or injured on the job (Powell & Tahan, 2010).

8. **C.**

The Worker Adjustment and Retraining Notification Act (WARN) offers protection to workers, their families, and their communities by mandating employers to give notice 60 days in advance of plant closing and mass layoffs. Enacted in 1988, this act requires employers to also give notice to workers' representatives (labor unions), to the State dislocated worker unit, and to the appropriate section of local government (U.S. Department of Labor, 2013).

9. **C.**

Under the Plant Closing section of the WARN provisions, a covered employer must give notice if an employment site will be shut down and this will result in an employment loss for more than 50 or more employees during a 30-day period (U.S. Department of Labor, 2013b).

10. **D.**

According to the Washington State Department of Labor Industries (2013), the criteria for admission to a work hardening program includes: physical recovery sufficient to permit progressive reactivation and participation for a minimum of four hours a day for three to five days a week; a defined return-to-work goal or documented on-the-job training ; the worker should be able to benefit from this program, documented by a screening review used to determine the likelihood of success; and the worker must be no more than two years past date of injury.

11. **A.**

The Job Accommodation Network (JAN) is a service provided by the Office of Disability Employment Policy of the U.S. Department of Labor. The mission of JAN is to encourage and assist with the employment and retention of workers with disabilities by providing information regarding job accommodations to employers, employment providers, people with disabilities, and other interested parties (Provine & Vierling, 2008).

12. **B.**

The Instrumental Activities of Daily Living (IADL) tool is used to evaluate patients with early-stage disease, to assess the level of the disease, and to determine the patient's ability to do self-care tasks. The IADL scale assesses the functional impact of cognitive, emotional, and physical impairments (Lawton & Brody, 1969). The functional capacity evaluation (FCE) is an instrument that reliably measures the functional physical ability of a person to perform work-related tasks (Chen, 2007). The Barthel Index of Activities of Daily Living tool measures functional disability by quantification of 10 activities of patient performance. The scoring system uses five-point increments with a maximum score of 100, indicating that the patient is fully independent in physical functioning (Mahoney & Barthel, 1965). The CAGE questionnaire assesses for alcohol use/abuse (Trigoboff, 2010).

13. **D.**

The Certification of Disability Management Specialists Commission (CDMSC) identifies three specific practice domains for disability management specialists. These are: disability case management, which involves specific tasks and knowledge to perform various tasks related to working with people who are injured, ill, or have a disability; disability prevention and workplace intervention, which brings together organizational and individual practice to identify how task and duties within disability management have formed and evolved, with responsibility to the individual and programs; and program development, management, and evaluation, which combines the administrative and managerial tasks that are the responsibility of the disability manager (Provine & Vierling, 2008).

14. **D.**

Durable medical equipment (DME) must be approved by the insurance company and ordered by one of the patient's physicians. The amount the beneficiary pays for equipment is based on what type of equipment is needed. Typically, after paying a $131 Medicare Part B deductible, the beneficiary may still have to pay for 20% co-insurance (Powell & Tahan, 2010).

15. **C.**

Durable medical equipment (DME) includes: basic mobility aids, such as canes, crutches, and walkers; assistive devices for independence with ADLs, such as shower chairs, hand rails, kitchen equipment, wound care supplies, and ostomy care supplies; mobility aids, such as electric beds and wheelchairs; and high-technology equipment, such as ventilators, IV pumps, infusion pumps, apnea/sleep monitors, and special electric beds. It does not include hearing aids and glasses (Powell & Tahan, 2010).

16. **D.**

17. **B.**

Ergonomics is a scientific discipline that is concerned with the interactions among humans and other elements of a system. It is the applied science of equipment design, which is intended to increase productivity by reducing operator discomfort and fatigue. Ergonomics is also called human factors engineering, human engineering, and biotechnology (Provine & Vierling, 2008).

18. **A.**

The Rehabilitation Act uses the definitions of assistive technology devices and services contained in the Assistive Technology for Individuals with Disabilities Act (AT Act). The term "assistive technology device" means any item, piece of equipment, or product system, whether acquired commercially off the shelf, modified, or customized, that is used to increase, maintain, or improve functional capabilities of individuals with disabilities. The term "assistive technology service" means any service that directly assists an individual with a disability in the selection, acquisition, or use of an assistive technology device (Hager, 2013).

19. **A.**

Occupational health case managers provide services that rely on the nature of the business setting, the philosophy of the case management program, and the expectations of the employer. In collaboration with other healthcare providers, these case managers coordinate the proactive efforts of the interdisciplinary team to facilitate the patient's healthcare services from the illness or injury onset to the end of case management services. Occupational health case managers serve as gatekeepers for rehabilitation, health services, and case management issues (Provine & Vierling, 2008).

20. **D.**

Disability case management is a process that follows various functions and activities, such as performing individual case analysis and benefits assessment, reviewing disability case management intervention protocols, collaborating with stakeholders, performing job analyses, developing return-to-work plans, implementing interventions, coordinating benefits and services, monitoring progress, and managing a caseload of clients. Disability managers are part of an interdisciplinary team involved in productivity improvement, benefit practice, and wellness programs (Provine & Vierling, 2008).

Made in the USA
Lexington, KY
09 March 2014